California Car Company

An Active Learning Costing Case

Steven J. Adams

Professor, California State University, Chico

LeRoy J. Pryor

Professor, California State University, Chico

THOMSON

SOUTH-WESTERN

California Car Company: An Active Learning Costing Case, 2e

Steven J. Adams, LeRoy J. Pryor

Editor-in-Chief:
Jack W. Calhoun

Team Leader:
Melissa S. Acuña

Acquisitions Editor:
Sharon Oblinger

Developmental Editor:
Sara E. Wilson

Marketing Manager:
Mignon Tucker

Production Editor:
Heather A. Mann

Manufacturing Coordinator:
Doug Wilke

Printer:
Globus Printing, Inc.
Minster, OH

Design Project Manager:
Rik Moore

Cover Design:
Rik Moore

Cover Photo Source:
PhotoDisc, Inc.

ISBN 0-324-18450-6

CALIFORNIA CAR COMPANY: AN ACTIVE LEARNING COSTING CASE

Table of Contents

PREFACE

The cases in this book are built around important, "real world" business decisions. Accounting issues arise as they are needed to address a specific decision. By learning accounting in a relevant decision context normally found in businesses, accounting will make more sense and should be more interesting and meaningful. In addition, learning theory predicts that information and concepts will be retained better if learned in a relevant context.

To illustrate the importance of context, consider the 2-point conversion strategy in football. Most coaches would agree that the 1-point conversion (kicking the ball through the goal posts) has a higher probability of success than the 2-point conversion (running or passing the ball into the end zone). Yet there are times when the coach will call for the 2-point conversion. To the observer who does not know the game of football, the 2-point strategy may not make sense due to a lack of context.

Suppose you were to describe to your friend, a football neophyte, a situation where Team A has just scored a touchdown and is one point ahead of Team B. There are two minutes left to play in the game and Team B has an excellent field goal kicker. Team A's coach must decide whether to go for the 1-point or 2-point conversion. You explain to your friend that if Team A makes the 1-point conversion followed by Team B making a field goal (three points) in the closing seconds of the game, Team A will lose by one point. Instead, if Team A makes the 2-point conversion followed by Team B's field goal, the score would be tied, giving Team A a chance to win in overtime. By providing the context, your friend is in a position to understand the rationale of the coach's decision to take the riskier 2-point strategy. Your friend would have a better understanding of the game of football than if you had just taught the rules.

To become effective economic decision makers in today's society, individuals must develop skills in the following three key areas:

Problem Solving—Enhancing analytical/problem-solving skills by engaging students in a variety of real world, unstructured problems that require problem definition and clarification, data collection, interpretation, analysis, and defense of proposed solutions.

Interpersonal—Improving abilities to communicate and to work together with others by engaging students in frequent writing exercises, oral presentations, and group activities.

Computer—Becoming more adept in the use of computers by engaging students in frequent computer applications in business, accounting, and economic decision-making activities.

The relevance of these skills to decision making is clear and immediate. First, the possession of creative problem-solving skills is obviously desirable. In business, economic decision problems neither present themselves in nicely structured, clearly defined terms; nor do they typically lead to well-defined solutions with a single, correct answer. Instead, real problems are ill-structured and "messy," and solutions often involve several defensible positions. Students need to recognize these complexities and gain practice in dealing with them. Cases provide an effective means for developing problem solving skills.

Second, most (if not all) significant economic decision-making activities involve interpersonal relationships. In real settings, problems are mostly addressed by teams rather than individuals. Problem analyses generally have to be communicated to others, both orally and in writing. Proposed courses of action may need to be vigorously defended in open debate or in position papers. Thus, it is clear that such interpersonal skills play a critical role in economic decision making. This case book includes several extensions of cases which require a group solution.

Finally, it should also be clear that computers, particularly personal computers, will play an increasing role in economic decision-making activities. The California Car Company case requires extensive use of spreadsheet software to organize analyses and to use sensitivity and "what if" analysis to assess decision risk.

Course Modules

The California Car Company case is divided into the following three modules:

1. Traditional Product Costing and Pricing

2. Cost Management Systems

3. Planning and Performance Evaluation in a Global Economy

Each module focuses on decision scenarios that students must address as the module progresses. These decision problems provide the context and rationale for studying related accounting and business subjects. The authors extend a warm welcome to you with the hope that you have a successful academic experience.

SUPPLEMENTS

Faculty Supplements

Instructor's manual. This book is a combination of an instructor's resource guide and a solutions manual. It is an excellent resource to help the instructor plan and teach the course. It provides specific instructions on how to organize unique features of the case, including two simulations and a structured controversy. The manual includes an overview of each case, teaching notes for each case, and suggested solutions to all cases.

Web site (www.csuchico.edu/acms/sadams_03). The web site for this book is an excellent resource for both faculty and students. Faculty can visit the site to secure electronic versions of case solutions to use as transparency masters. The site also contains an updated matrix showing the sections of each popular managerial and cost text that correspond with each California Car Company case assignment.

Self-grading templates. New with the second edition are templates that automatically grade key quantitative check figures in the case. As the students complete a part of the case, the template will indicate whether they computed the correct number. The templates are constructed so that if a student is unable to get one number correct, the student can continue on and will get credit for the correct formulas (logic) later in the case even if the number itself is incorrect due to an earlier error. These templates have been class-tested for a year in Chico and have been very well received by students. In fact, students are disappointed when we do a case that doesn't have a self-graded template. Chico assessment data are available upon request. This feature also makes the cases easy to grade.

Simulation video. An instructional video in VCR format showing how to run the first simulation is available from the authors upon request. E-mail Steve Adams at sjadams@csuchico.edu for information.

Toy blocks for the simulation. Toy blocks are available from South-Western for use in the simulations. Please check the faculty portion of the book's web site for details on how to obtain the blocks.

Student Supplements

Web site (www.csuchico.edu/acms/sadams_03). Students find the web site to be a very important resource for this book. The wide variety of items contained in the site include:

1. Helpful hints for completing the case assignments, including check figures,

2. A simulation video accessed with RealPlayer,

3. Downloadable spreadsheet templates for selected cases, and

4. Excel spreadsheet instructions.

Students should visit this site regularly to see what new materials may have been added.

Acknowledgments

The original concept for the California Car company was derived from a Fund for the Improvement of Post Secondary Education (FIPSE) grant from the U.S. Department of Education to the accounting faculty at California State University, Chico. We thank the U.S. Department of Education for their confidence in us and our research concept and also to the following Chico faculty who were originally involved in developing much of this material: Sally L. Adams, Curtis L. DeBerg, Wesley E. Harder, Donald E. Keller, Paul Krause, and Richard B. Lea. We also gratefully acknowledge the contributions of the following persons who have shared ideas and comments on various parts of the materials:

Sherri Anderson	Sonoma State University
Angele Brill	Castleton State College
Janet Cassagio	Nassau Community College
Dianna Coker	St. Mary's University
Joe Colgan	Fort Lewis College
Jack Flanagan	Australian Catholic University
Glenn W. Goodale	Castleton State College
Bob Harrington	Fort Lewis College
Mary Harston	St. Mary's University
Norma C. Holter	Towson State University
Lynn Mazzola	Nassau Community College
Tom Madison	St. Mary's University
Sue Ravenscroft	Iowa State University
Patrick Reihing	Nassau Community College
Alan Taylor	Australian Catholic University

We are indebted to the following persons for their help in putting this manuscript together: Mildred Adams, Sally Adams, and Sandy Jensen. We also thank the Accounting and Tax Team of South-Western Thomson Learning for their hard work and dedication. And, finally we thank our families for their encouragement, patience and support in this labor of love.

Steve Adams
Lee Pryor

California Car Company Case Student Information Sheet	Class Section

All requested information other than name and internet address is optional	
Name	Phone

E-mail address:

Year (Freshman, Sophomore, Junior, Senior, Graduate)   Gender   M ❑   F ❑

Other colleges attended:	From	To

Proposed major or concentration (e.g., English, math, marketing, etc.):   Cumulative GPA:

Is English your first language?   Yes ❑   No ❑

Level of spreadsheet (Excel, etc.) proficiency?   High ❑   Moderate ❑   Low ❑

Prior Bookkeeping, Accounting, and Math Courses Taken

Course title	Date Taken	Where Taken	Instructor	Grade

Is your commute to campus more than 10 miles?   Yes ❑   No ❑   If yes, please indicate city or town from which you commute:

Briefly describe any prior business-related work experience that you have acquired (clerical, sales, warehousing, bookkeeping, etc.):

Briefly indicate any career plans that you intend to pursue or are thinking about pursuing:

Do you have a seating preference in this classroom? If so, where?

MODULE ONE

TRADITIONAL PRODUCT

Costing and Pricing

INTRODUCTION TO
CALIFORNIA CAR COMPANY
AND ITS ENVIRONMENT

INTRODUCTION

The purpose of this reading is to introduce the hybrid gasoline-electric vehicle industry, provide you with an overview of a hybrid vehicle production company, discuss manufacturing processes that add value for customers (value chain), and to define the type of accounting terminology used in the manufacturing environment. The reading describes California Car Company's (CCC) production structure and cost accounting system. CCC is a car manufacturing company that builds low-emission vehicles (LEVs). The management of this company, entrepreneurs at heart, has experience in auto manufacturing and envisions a great future for hybrid vehicles. The content of this reading should help you understand the importance and purpose of appropriate accounting information, define basic accounting terms that you will use in preparing cost data reports for CCC decision making, and supply the necessary background on CCC to help you answer the Requirements of Case 1-1. The reading also provides necessary background information to prepare you for the production simulation in Case 1-2.

THE HYBRID VEHICLE INDUSTRY

The internal combustion engine, using gasoline or diesel fuel, has not been the only means to supply power to vehicles. Many of the early cars that traveled the roads in the first decades of the last century were electric or steam powered. In 1897, the biggest selling model in motor vehicles was electric. Electric streetcars and buses were also common sights at one time in many U.S. cities, and San Francisco still has numerous electric buses in service. The higher production and operating costs, however, limited traveling range, inconvenience, and poor acceleration that characterized electric vehicles quickly triggered a loss in their popularity. Steam engines proved to be inferior to gasoline-powered cars as they used more petroleum plus large amounts of water. Disadvantages of both the electric and steam vehicles led to the almost universal domination of gasoline and diesel cars that were faster, cheaper, more convenient, and, from an engineering perspective, more adaptable to technological improvements.

Gasoline engines were not without disadvantages. Studies showed that motor vehicles were a major source of air pollution, which surfaced as a major ecological and societal concern during the final quarter of the twentieth century. Clearly, a need had arisen for an alternative to the internal combustion engine. Lack of success in developing convenient storage batteries and inconsistent operating capability of steam vehicles indicated that the alternative to the gasoline car needed to be something other than the electric or steam-powered motor. Despite the post World War II interest in auto technological innovation, inventors had not seriously thought of combining electricity and gasoline to fuel cars with reduced pollution emissions. Now, however, the need to squeeze more miles out of a gallon of gasoline has produced the hybrid vehicles.

Current Market Situation

Today's drivers want vehicles that maintain speed in traffic with a range of at least 300 miles between refuelings. The gasoline-powered car meets this criteria but produces pollution and gets low mileage per gallon. Most users, however, only need an engine large enough to accelerate and perform at peak capability less than one percent of road time. A smaller engine would run more efficiently, weigh less, and require less fuel. The hybrid gasoline-electric engine provides advantages over both the solely electric and solely gasoline-fueled vehicle. The hybrid has both an electric motor and battery and a gasoline engine, but utilizes only one energy system, electric or gasoline, for routine travel and the second to provide the "burst" of power necessary for acceleration and special situations.

Currently, only two car manufacturers, Toyota and Honda, produce hybrid gasoline-electric vehicles for sale in the United States. The Honda Insight was first introduced in the United States in 2000.   The Insight has the better mileage of the two and drives like a conventional car because of the highly efficient gasoline engine, but it is a small two-seater. The Toyota Prius was introduced in 1997, is a four-door sedan that seats five people, and is about the size of a Toyota Corolla. Because the car can use its electric motor to maintain a speed of 15 mph without the gasoline engine kicking in, it is more environmentally conscious than the Honda Insight. An additional advantage to the Prius is that its batteries never need recharging since a built-in generator accomplishes that task.

As mentioned in the previous section, purely electric alternative vehicles to the gasoline car are uncompetitive for cost and performance reasons. The small number that are sold or leased are primarily tiny electric commuter cars with very limited range and power, or retrofitted traditional cars and vans that are much more expensive than their gasoline-powered relatives. The two market sectors in which electric vehicles compete successfully are the golf cart and U.S. postal service mail delivery vehicle segments. In a way, these successes have hindered the industry because they have led to a public perception of electric vehicles as novelty or specialty items, more like toys than means of serious highway transportation.

Future Demand

The future of alternative vehicles, powered by non-gasoline sources, was changed radically in 1990 by the California Air Resources Board. This state agency set a 1998 target that two percent of all new cars sold in California (about 40,000 cars) be zero-emission vehicles (ZEVs). It also mandated that in the year 2000 5 percent (about 100,000) of all new cars be ZEVs. The original year 2003 requirements for ZEVs were 10 percent (about 200,000) of all cars sold. In addition, after California's action several other states, such as New York and Massachusetts, representing almost 40 percent of the market for new cars, indicated that they would take similar action. Large automotive manufacturers began designing concept electric cars during the 1990s. General Motor's eye-catching EV1 celebrated its first birthday in December 1997, and has been redesigned and improved during the last five years.

Standards have been relaxed somewhat in recent years, indicating the need for LEVs rather than vehicles that are totally free of pollution emissions. For instance, California regulators have recommended lowering the 2003 goal of 10 percent ZEVs to two percent and substituting a requirement for 8 percent hybrid vehicles. This could mean that within the next ten years the demand for LEVs in the United States could approach one million cars per year.   Although there are other experimental nonhybrid LEVs, such as the experimental hydrogen-powered cars, from a practical perspective, environmental requirements for LEVs will mean hybrid gasoline-electric vehicles for the foreseeable future. As a result, global auto makers such as DaimlerChrysler, Ford, and General Motors, in addition to Toyota and Honda, all have projects underway to develop attractive hybrid vehicles. Ford Motor Company plans to release its hybrid electric SUV, the Escape, in 2003. DaimlerChrysler also is working on a hybrid version of its Dodge Durango SUV plus a concept hybrid electric vehicle, the Citadel. Additionally, the large car manufacturers, DaimlerChrysler, Ford, and General Motors, established an association in 1992 called the United States Council for Automotive Research (USCAR) to jointly develop improved LEV technology. In an effort to accelerate the development of environmentally clean vehicles, the U.S. government joined this group in 1993 to form the Partners for a New Generation of Vehicles (PNGV) that continues as the cooperative global organization for LEV research.

Despite the interest of the world's major auto companies, many believe that because the technology is still immature and because the hybrid vehicle is significantly different, there is room in the industry for smaller, entrepreneurial companies.

STRATEGY OF CALIFORNIA CAR COMPANY

CCC's overall strategy is to use the flexibility and diligence of a small company to establish and maintain a technology and quality advantage in the marketplace. CCC plans to appeal to consumers who are interested in quality and special features. They do not plan to compete head on with the major auto manufacturers in the mass market for hybrid vehicles. CCC views themselves as more like a Volvo than a Ford or Toyota. The development of a compact hybrid car is a natural result of this strategy. Although more expensive than a traditional hybrid compact, this car will appeal to consumers who want a sporty-looking model, but who are still environmentally sensitive.

Marketing strategy is a critical part of CCC's plans. CCC hopes to develop an environmentally aware, high-quality image. As a result, CCC plans to price their products at or a little above average, but hopes customers will perceive that the extra features of its cars are worth much more than the increased price. If all goes well, CCC will build a loyal following of customers who will make repeat purchases. Ideally, a kind of "cult following" will develop similar to Volkswagon's bug. A second aspect of CCC's marketing plan is to reach an agreement with a major auto company such as Toyota or Honda, whereby another auto company would sell CCC cars under its nameplate. Such an agreement would give CCC access to a huge dealer network.

HISTORY OF CCC AND ITS MANAGEMENT STRUCTURE

The purpose of this section is to give you an idea of how CCC came into being and the background that might be representative of the top managers in an entrepreneurial manufacturing firm like CCC. The company initially was established as a research and development organization and gradually was transformed into the operating company that exists today. CCC is divided into the following four administrative areas, each of which is headed by a vice president (see Exhibit I-1):

- Production
- Marketing
- Finance
- Engineering

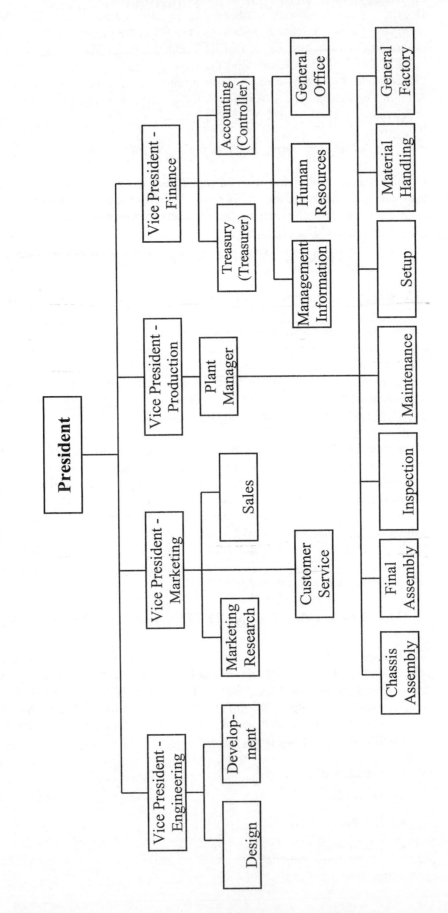

Exhibit I-1
California Car Company Organization Chart

David Gomez—President of California Car Company

David graduated with a bachelor's degree in engineering from St. Mary's University in San Antonio, Texas, and went to work for General Dynamics, a large aerospace firm. David worked in the quality control area and after six years was named plant manager of quality control. After two years in this position, David decided that he wanted to move into a higher management position. Therefore, he left General Dynamics and enrolled in the manufacturing management master of business administration program at the Massachusetts Institute of Technology. After graduation, David accepted a position as assistant plant manager at General Motors (GM) in Lordstown, Ohio. Four years later he was promoted to plant manager at GM's Fremont, California, plant.

Shortly after his arrival at Fremont, GM entered into negotiations with Toyota to establish a joint venture called New United Motor Manufacturing, Inc. (NUMMI). Meshing the Toyota and GM way of manufacturing cars was a tremendous challenge, but also an incredible learning experience. David spent a considerable amount of time in Japan being trained in Toyota's production philosophy. He likens this experience to earning a Ph.D. in production management. Five years later David was named vice president of production for NUMMI.

The production management system at NUMMI was a smashing success. NUMMI took what was GM's least productive and least automated factory and kept what was universally considered to be GM's worst factory labor force. Within a couple of years, with very little new equipment investment, NUMMI became GM's most productive plant with the best labor relations.

Despite NUMMI's success, David was becoming restless. For one thing, he had become intrigued with the prospects of the electric or hybrid electric/gas vehicle industry. It appeared to him that by 1998 environmental and legal forces, particularly in California, would catapult vehicles that did not rely solely on the gasoline engine to the status of a major industry. David had tried to interest GM in transferring him to its electric vehicle development group, but without success. Secondly, David had always dreamed of starting his own business and being his own boss. David began discussing his interest in forming a hybrid vehicle company with Sally Swanson, production manager at NUMMI, over a few after-work beers. Sally also was enthusiastic about hybrid vehicles and was very excited at the prospect of starting a company.

David and Sally, with their personal funds, hired a consulting firm to prepare a business plan. The manager in charge of their business plan, Jena Butler, took a special interest in their project and put them in contact with a large venture capital partnership she had done work for in the past. Much to David and Sally's surprise, the venture capital firm liked their idea and initially put up $3,500,000 and eventually invested a total of $14,000,000. The agreement left David and Sally with a combined 30 percent ownership in CCC.

As president, David has final responsibility for the performance of the entire company; this includes hiring and evaluating the top managers and solving major problems that arise. Second, he reports CCC's performance, prospects and problems to the board of directors, venture capitalists, and bankers. Third, he is involved in negotiations with major customers, vendors, and the union. David must use accounting reports extensively in performing his duties. For example, he must assess the performance of CCC and its managers based partially on financial reports. He must present CCC's financial position to the board and to others, and he must negotiate prices with major customers and vendors based on cost accounting information.

Sally Swanson—Vice President of Production

Sally graduated from Baylor University in Waco, Texas, with a bachelor of science in business with a concentration in production and operations management. After graduation, she took a position with GM as a production management trainee. After three years as an assistant manager, she was named manager of the Transmission Assembly Department. In this capacity she oversaw 150 employees who produced about $125,000,000 worth of transmissions per year.

During her fourth year as manager, Sally became interested in moving up to a higher management position, and realized that an MBA from a top school would enhance her prospects significantly. Therefore, Sally left GM after four years and enrolled in the Stanford MBA program. After receiving her MBA, Sally accepted a position as assistant plant manager at New United Motors Manufacturing, Inc. (NUMMI), the General Motors-Toyota joint venture in Fremont, California. This position required that Sally support the plant manager in a wide array of tasks, including investigating and recommending solutions for problems in production scheduling, quality, bottlenecks, and cost areas. Her most important assignment, however, was to oversee the continuous improvement efforts of work groups in NUMMI's just-in-time environment.

During Sally's third year at NUMMI, the position of production manager opened up and her previous hard work was rewarded with a promotion to that job. In her second year as production manager, Sally left NUMMI for the opportunity to help form an exciting new company that planned to produce hybrid vehicles: California Car Company.

Sally is responsible for hiring and evaluating the performance of all department managers in the manufacturing area. She has final responsibility for the plant design and purchase of equipment for the plant. She also oversees a staff responsible for scheduling production, assuring quality, reporting manufacturing accounting information, and purchasing parts and materials from vendors.

George Olson—Vice President of Marketing

George received his bachelor of science degree in engineering from Colorado State University in Fort Collins, Colorado, and went to work at Ford Motor Co. in the product design area. After two years at Ford, George decided that he really enjoyed marketing and sales more than product development. Therefore, he left Ford and enrolled in the MBA program at the University of Michigan.

Upon receipt of his MBA, George took a sales position with Eaton Corp., a large auto parts supplier. After eight years at Eaton, George moved up to marketing manager for a major division. George saw great potential in the hybrid vehicle industry. Consequently, he devoted considerable time in trying to establish a partnership between Eaton and CCC because he thought that CCC might grow to be a major Eaton customer. The more George talked to David Gomez and Sally Swanson, the more excited he became about CCC's prospects. As a result, when George was offered the vice president of marketing position, he accepted without hesitation.

George's major responsibilities at CCC are to develop a marketing strategy, to hire and train a sales force, and to oversee the development of a dealer network. George also is heavily involved in pricing decisions, in presenting customer needs in design decisions, and in advertising decisions.

Jena Butler—Vice President of Finance

Jena Butler received a bachelor of science in accounting and a bachelor of arts in history from Castleton State College in Castleton, Vermont. She started college as a history major, but decided it was prudent to take a few business courses to enhance her job prospects. She enjoyed using computers, and to her surprise liked the introductory accounting courses. Jena then took the intermediate and cost accounting courses and declared a second major in that field. After graduation, she accepted a position as a staff auditor in a Big Six (now the Big Five) international accounting firm. After four years and a promotion to senior auditor, Jena decided she preferred a career in consulting.

She took a two-year leave of absence and enrolled in the master of science in accountancy program at California State University in Chico. This program emphasized the accounting applications of information technology and production management. Upon graduation she returned to the same accounting firm, although in the management consulting area of the San Francisco office.

For the next several years Jena worked extensively with venture capital firms in helping fast-growth, high-tech companies solve their accounting and production systems problems. This work with entrepreneurs and new ventures created an interest in participating in a start-up company as a manager and part owner rather than as a consultant. Jena received several employment offers from clients, but none of them felt right until, after supervising the development of a business plan for CCC, she was offered the position of vice president of finance and an ownership stake. Although partnership in the accounting firm and a $250,000 annual salary seemed imminent, she quickly accepted CCC's offer.

Jena is responsible for all the external report preparation, including CCC's financial statements, tax reports, and other regulatory filings. She hires and evaluates the performance of the treasurer, controller, management information systems director, manager of human resources, and the office manager. Jena, and the cost analysts that work for her, work closely with all other CCC managers and provide information needed to make decisions. The other top managers view her as an internal consultant to be called in when major decisions are made. She spends much of her time planning and overseeing the implementation of CCC's management information systems. Note that the controller of a firm is the person with the responsibility for ensuring that all events affecting CCC are properly recorded and reflected in the financial statements. The treasurer is the person responsible for the control of the firm's assets, including cash, inventory, and machinery.

PHYSICAL STRUCTURE OF CCC

Because CCC began as a research and development company then evolved into a manufacturing concern, the physical structure of the facilities was not planned with an eye for the future of automotive manufacturing or the storage of inventory. This layout evolved through time, with new activities being assigned to vacant space as they were created. The physical layout of the production and operations facility for CCC is shown in Exhibit I-2.

Plant Layout

Building 1, the original facility, now contains all administrative, marketing and finance functions, as well as certain engineering and production functions such as the final assembly, inspection, maintenance and setup, finished goods (outgoing) inventory storage and shipping activities, and engineering. Building 2 houses all other production activities, including receiving, parts inventory storage, chassis assembly, and various other production support functions. The plant layout diagram is drawn to scale. Notice that assembly and inventory storage together occupy more than 50 percent of the total manufacturing space.

Production Process

The plant layout described represents a traditional, departmentalized **production process** that manufactures both CCC sedan and compact models. A production process is a sequence of events involved in the manufacturing activities necessary to complete a product, including the delivery of materials and the cutting, assembly, finishing, and inspection of units. The administration of CCC production is divided into seven manufacturing responsibility centers—two assembly departments and five overhead departments. A **responsibility center** is a unit of an organization that holds its manager accountable for specific activities and outcomes that may include costs, revenues, or profits. The production departments are Chassis Assembly and Final Assembly. Inspection, Maintenance, Setup, Material Handling, and General Factory are classified as overhead departments. As Exhibit I-2 indicates, production begins in the Chassis Assembly Department.

Inventories

From chassis assembly, unfinished vehicles move to work-in-process inventory storage where they are then drawn into final assembly as needed. **Work-in-process inventory** consists of all partially completed units. After final assembly, completed units pass through inspection and then to outgoing storage called finished goods inventory where they stay until shipped to customers. **Finished goods inventory** contains all the completed units waiting to be sold or shipped to customers.

Work-in-process and finished goods are not the only inventories in manufacturing. All incoming parts are received and inspected in the Receiving Department. After inspection, parts are moved by material handlers to inventory storage, called the **materials inventory**, to await their use in chassis or final assembly. The Materials Inventory Storage Department maintains an adequate stock of all parts needed for the production of sedans and compacts. Parts quantities are monitored through the use of computerized economic order quantity (EOQ) models. EOQ models signal to purchasing managers when to order parts and how many parts to order at one time. Management is quite proud that parts inventory and ordering have been automated. A list of parts used in the manufacture of sedans and compacts appears in Case 1-1.

THE MANUFACTURING VALUE CHAIN

CCC's strategy to achieve flexibility and an advantage in the marketplace requires management to concentrate on improving quality at all levels of the company's operations. Ensuring quality necessitates the establishment of a **value chain** that optimizes the use of resources and promotes the efficient exchange of information. An organization's value chain consists of the set of interdependent processes that adds value to a product or service provided to customers. **Value-added activities** are those processes that increase customer satisfaction and enhance quality. These activities also may reduce delivery times and/or reduce prices charged for products and services. In contrast, *nonvalue-added* activities may exist that accomplish none of these things and most likely increase sales prices. Therefore, once identified, they should be eliminated. Note that value is essentially a *customer-oriented* concept. In this context, value should be measured in terms of nonfinancial goals, such as reduced defects, as well as more traditional financial measures, such as price.

Exhibit I-2
California Car Company
Traditional Plant Layout

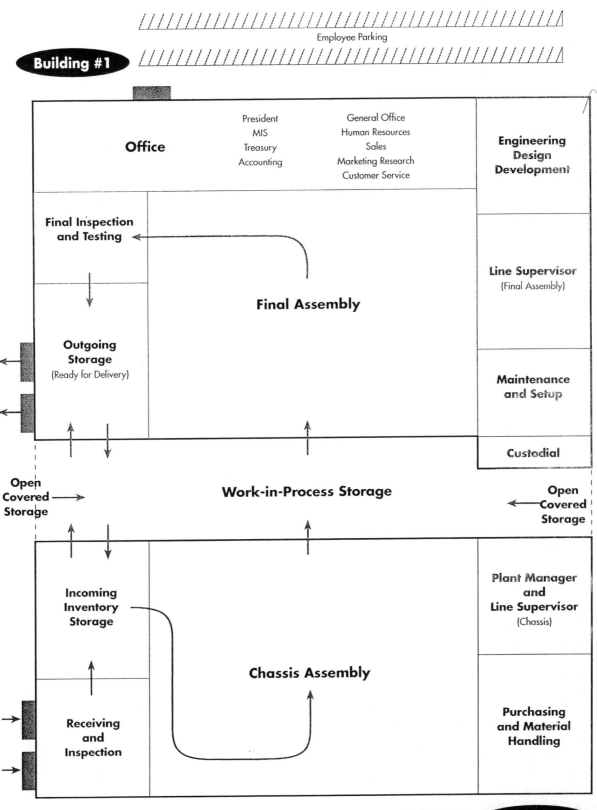

A value-added focus is of great importance to all organizations striving to be competitive in today's global economy. As a newcomer to this competitive market, CCC is well aware of today's emphasis on quality and is in the process of identifying the value-added activities within its own organization structure. The company has identified the following major activities as comprising its value chain illustrated in Exhibit I-3:

- Research and development,
- Product design,
- Production,
- Marketing,
- Distribution, and
- Customer service.

Exhibit I-3
Manufacturing Value Chain

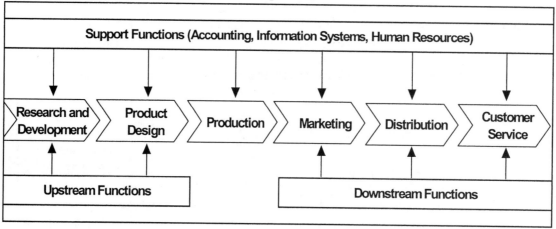

Extending the Value Chain Concept Beyond Company Boundaries: An Example from the Business World

The concept of a value chain may be extended beyond the boundaries of a particular company. For example, in the case of CCC, lying "upstream" are suppliers of raw materials and parts and delivery companies bringing those items to the company. Likewise, lying "downstream" are auto dealers and finally, at the end of the line, the customers of the dealers. Value can be added to CCC's vehicles at any step in this comprehensive value chain, which includes both internal and external activities. An example from the Hewlett-Packard (HP), Roseville, California, operation illustrates how a value chain can be extended to units outside the company.

HP defines its internal value-added operation as the assembly of component parts and the delivery of a finished product. The company made major efforts to farm out the manufacture of component parts. Consequently, nonrelated companies at distant locations now manufacture many parts. HP works very closely with only a few parts suppliers to ensure quality and timely delivery of parts.

HP even has gone so far as to work out changes in delivery packaging with its unrelated trucking firm to eliminate nonvalue-added costs. HP receives molded plastic cases from a firm in Oregon. In the past, cases were packaged in cardboard cartons to prevent marring during shipment. Upon arrival at HP, the cartons were removed, folded, and sent back to the supplying firm. Notice that handling of the cardboard cartons is a good example of a nonvalue-added activity. Once a nonvalue-added activity is identified, management can work towards elimination of that activity and its related cost, which is exactly what HP did. Working with both the manufacturer of the plastic cases and the trucking firm, HP developed a method of shipping the plastic cases without any additional packaging, eliminating the need for and handling of the nonvalue-added shipping carton.

A second example of external value chain analysis involves the following problem recently addressed by HP. Trucks were arriving full at the HP plant, but had no designated loads for the return trip to Oregon. The trucks often made the return trip empty. This deadheading of returns was a cost that was indirectly being passed on to HP through the shipping charge for plastic cases. Realizing this was a nonvalue-added activity being performed externally, HP worked with the trucker and found return loads from another HP supplier. The net result of this value chain analysis was that HP was happy because of the lower cost of their one-way shipments, the supplier was happy because it found a reliable and low cost shipper, and the trucking company was happy because it now had two-way loads and increased revenue.

These examples illustrate that managers, who expand their views of value-added activities beyond the traditional production-oriented emphasis, may realize substantial gains. The examples also suggest that the types of information useful to managers who are involved in value chain analyses must be considerably broader than the financial information contained in a traditional income statement.

ACCOUNTING FOR MANUFACTURING

Before managers can make beneficial decisions that determine value-added activities, they must have a basic understanding of production flow and the cost terminology associated with manufacturing. The cost accounting system at CCC was originally designed to provide information to management about product costs for the purpose of valuing the year-end inventories of parts, work-in-process, and finished goods. As production volume increased, managers found it increasingly difficult to keep track of activities by direct observation. Consequently, the cost accounting system gradually has been modified to produce monthly "responsibility center" reports that allow management to evaluate performance at various operating levels. The cost accounting system at CCC measures the following three inputs to the manufacturing process and combines them to determine product costs for the sedan and compact:

- Direct materials
- Direct labor
- Manufacturing overhead

Direct Costs

Direct material and direct labor costs occur only in the Chassis Assembly and Final Assembly departments. **Direct material** represents the cost of parts that are included in the cars. **Direct labor** cost represents the pay of production workers who work assembling vehicles or vehicle components. Each assembly department has a supervisor who is responsible for the operation of that department and the control of direct material and direct labor costs. Departments in which direct material and direct labor occur are termed **production departments**.

Manufacturing Overhead Costs

Manufacturing overhead consists of all remaining manufacturing costs that are incurred in producing the LEVs. These are indirect in that they represent the costs for manufacturing activities that, while necessary, do not physically or directly affect the produced unit. As shown in Exhibit I-4, CCC has created the following overhead departments into which all manufacturing costs, other than direct material and direct labor, are collected:

- *Inspection*—All costs of inspecting cars and fixing defective ones. Repairing defects discovered before products leave the factory is known as rework.

- *Maintenance*—All costs of fixing and maintaining equipment, including salaries and parts, plus all equipment depreciation charges.

- *Setup*—All costs of changing the factory equipment to switch production from one model to another.

- *Material Handling*—All costs of ordering and receiving parts and materials, of loading cars on trucks, and moving work-in-process inventory in the plant.

- *General Factory*—All other manufacturing costs including building occupancy costs, plant support costs such as cost accounting and manufacturing engineering, and plant management.

Exhibit I-4
California Car Company
Flow of Costs to the Income Statement

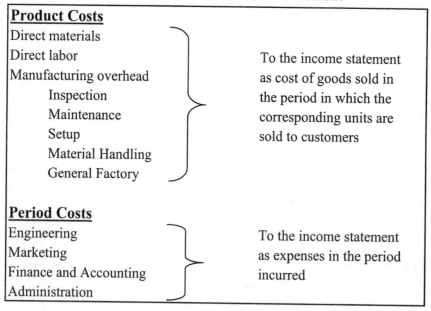

Manufacturing overhead costs initially are collected in the overhead departments and the overhead department managers have primary responsibility for controlling these costs. Overhead costs eventually are allocated to each car manufactured. The Chassis and Final Assembly department managers are responsible for controlling the total manufacturing cost.

Note that all costs incurred in the various production departments are considered to be **product costs** and therefore can be included in inventory. When units of production are sold, these costs appear as cost of goods sold on the income statement. Conversely, all marketing and administration costs, including engineering, are considered to be **period costs** and are therefore recognized as expenses in the period incurred. Exhibit I-4 summarizes the company's cost flows and shows how they enter into the yearly measurement of net income. Product costs for all partially completed goods not yet sold are collected in the work-in-process inventory account. The cost of completed, but unsold, goods remains in the finished goods inventory account. Costs at the end of an accounting period for all three inventories—materials, work-in-process, and finished goods—appear on the balance sheet.

SUMMARY

The reading first furnishes a brief description of the hybrid vehicle industry and introduces CCC and its top management in order to provide you with a background for the case assignments of Module 1. CCC's elements of a manufacturing value chain are identified, their importance explained, and an example of a value chain concept from the real business world is presented.

EXERCISES AND PROBLEMS

Exercises

Exercise 1 Demand for Cars. Discuss why the gasoline or internal combustion engine has become the favorite of motorists over alternative forms of power. Also discuss why future demand for a hybrid vehicle may be increasing.

Exercise 2 CCC's Strategy. List CCC's four primary goals to meet the current market situation in the vehicle industry.

Exercise 3 Advantages of Motor Vehicles. Indicate whether each of the following items is an advantage of a gasoline-powered vehicle (g) or an advantage of an electric-powered vehicle (e) or is not relevant (n) to the comparison of gasoline with electric-powered vehicles.

a.   Longer traveling range
b.   Adequate maintenance of speed in traffic
c.   High mileage per unit of power
d.   Convenience of operation
e.   Less expensive to manufacture
f.   Accelerates easily
g.   More environmentally friendly
h.   Adaptable to technological improvements
i.   Consistency of operation
j.   Uses large amounts of water

Exercise 4 Disadvantages of Motor Vehicles. Indicate whether each of the following items is a disadvantage of a gasoline-powered vehicle (g) or a disadvantage of an electric-powered vehicle (e) or is not relevant (n) to the comparison of gasoline with electric-powered vehicles.

a.   Limited traveling range
b.   Slow acceleration
c.   Costly to manufacture

d. Source of air pollution
e. Inconsistent operating ability
f. Bulky storage of power supply
g. Low mileage per unit of power
h. Frequent refueling
i. Uses large amounts of water
j. Difficulty in adapting to technological improvements

Exercise 5 Responsibilities of CCC Management Positions. Indicate whether each of the following officer job responsibilities belongs to the position of the president (p), the vice president of finance (vf), or does not apply to either officer (n). If the responsibility applies to both positions, write (p) and (vf) as your answer.

a. Oversees the preparation of all external reports including the financial statements— *VF*
b. Hires and evaluates top officers— P
c. Hires and evaluates the treasurer, controller, and management information systems director — *VF*
d. Oversees the development of a dealer network— *N*
e. Reports the company performance and financial position to the board of directors — *P*
f. Negotiates prices with major customers and vendors— P
g. Schedules production— *N*
h. Uses accounting information — *VF, P*
i. Controls the firm's assets — *VF*
j. Controls the recording and reflection of events in the financial statements— *VF*
k. Works closely with cost accountants and other CCC managers to provide relevant information for decision making. — *VF*

Exercise 6 Responsibilities of CCC Management Positions. Indicate whether each of the following officer job responsibilities belongs to the position of the vice president of marketing (vm), vice president of production (vp), or does not apply to either officer (n). If the responsibility applies to both positions, write (vm) and (vp) as your answer.

a. Oversees the preparation of all external reports including the financial statements— *N*
b. Hires and evaluates managers of manufacturing— *Vp*
c. Hires and trains the sales force — *Vm*
d. Oversees the development of a dealer network— *Vm*
e. Makes final decision for plant design— *VP*
f. Negotiates prices with major customers and vendors— *N*
g. Schedules production— *VP*
h. Uses accounting information— *VP, Vm*
i. Involved in pricing, customer needs, and advertising decisions— *Vm*
j. Controls the recording and reflection of events in the financial statements— *N*
k. Oversees the purchasing of parts and materials — *VP*

Exercise 7 CCC's Responsibility Centers. List CCC's manufacturing responsibility centers. State which are production departments and which are overhead centers.

Exercise 8 Activities Classification in a Value Chain. Component costs of a value chain may represent activities that extend beyond the boundaries of a particular company or production department. For each of the following items, indicate (u) for those costs or activities that would occur upstream of the production function, (d) for those that would occur downstream of the production function, and (n) for neither upstream or downstream costs of activities.

a. Drawing blueprints for a new model car - U
b. Repairing a dishwasher sold to a customer the previous year - D
c. Choosing the product to manufacture that will maintain a lucrative competitive advantage - U
d. Testing a prototype (model) of a product - U
e. Putting the final coat of paint on a car product - N
f. Hiring market representatives – D
g. Running initial laboratory tests on an antibiotic produced by a pharmaceutical company - U
h. Paying commissions to the sales force of a manufacturing company - D
i. Adding steel doors to a car on an assembly line - N
j. Delivering a dishwasher to a customer's home. D

Exercise 9   Product Value. Assume that you just purchased a new car. List three items involved with the car purchase that did not add value. State why each of your stated three items did not add value.

Exercise 10   Product Value. For each of the following items state two elements of value that the product supplies.

a. Recently released movie
b. Car
c. Television set
d. College night course
e. Fast-food meal
f. Off-campus apartment
g. Dormitory room
h. Campus cafeteria
i. Business suit
j. CD player

Exercise 11   Activity Value. Indicate whether each of the following activities from the customer's perspective adds value (a) or does not add value (n).

a. Storage of Work-in-process inventory - n
b. Product design - a
c. Inspection - a
d. Defect-free manufacturing - a
e. Quick delivery - a
f. Accounting - n
g. Product marketing - a
h. Human Resources employee support - n
i. Warranty service - a
j. Machine repair - n
   of Equipment

Exercise 12   Lack of Value. For each of the following items provide one product characteristic that does not add value.

a. Recently released movie
b. Car
c. Television set
d. College night course
e. Fast-food meal
f. Off-campus apartment

g. Dormitory room
h. Campus cafeteria
i. Business suit
j. CD player

Exercise 13 Product Versus Period Cost Classification. Classify each of the following costs as product (pro) or period costs (per).

a. Wages of material handlers
b. Wages for painters of cars working on an assembly line
c. Replacement bits for drilling machines used to manufacture products
d. Product advertising on television
e. Utility bill for management offices
f. Shipping clerk wages
g. Salary for vice president of production
h. Fire insurance for office building
i. Salaries for engineers that design new computer programs for a software manufacturing company
j. Ground meat patties in a fast-food restaurant

Exercise 14 Product Versus Period Cost Classification. Classify each of the following costs as product (pro) or period (per) costs.

a. Sales commissions
b. Setup labor wages
c. President's salary
d. Rent for factory
e. Utility bill for employee parking lot
f. Milk used to produce butter
g. Depreciation on the building wing that houses production
h. Salary for financial accountant who helps the company treasurer prepare financial statements
i. Paint for cars made on an assembly line
j. Inspector's wages

Exercise 15 Cost Classification. Classify each of the following costs as direct materials (dm), direct labor (dl), manufacturing overhead (moh), or not a product cost (n).

a. Sales commissions
b. Setup labor wages
c. Assembly line worker wages
d. Rent for factory
e. Utility bill for factory machines
f. Milk used to produce butter
g. Depreciation on the building wing that houses production
h. Paper to record cost accounting records for manufacturing
i. Paint for cars made on an assembly line
j. Inspector's wages

Case 1-1

CALIFORNIA CAR COMPANY BACKGROUND

Case Objective

1. Introduce students to the products and financial statements of California Car Company.

INTRODUCTION TO CCC

California Car Company (CCC) is planning for its tenth year of business, year 2002. The company was formed in 1992 by a group of engineers and business people formerly associated with NUMMI.[1] The company manufactures two models of hybrid gas and electric vehicles. The company has one established model, a sedan-sized vehicle, and has developed a second, compact-sized model to fill the anticipated market demand for smaller vehicles. The compact model, which was introduced in 2000, incorporates solar panels (not included in the sedan) to lower its operating costs and increase miles per gallon. CCC's year 2002 capacity is 30 vehicles per day (single shift), or about 7,500 vehicles a year. CCC can increase its annual production through the use of overtime or by adding a second shift.

Bill of Materials

A list of the parts used in the manufacture of a product is called a **bill of materials**. It normally includes the quantity of each type of part used, as well as department or factory area in which the part is used. The price of each part is often included in the bill of materials so that the cost of materials for each product manufactured can be determined readily. The bill of materials for CCC is shown as Exhibit 1-1.1. The bill of material parts correspond to the toy blocks shown in Exhibit 1-2.2. If your school uses a different type of toy block, the bill of material will not match your blocks. Regardless of the type of blocks used at your school, use the number of parts and cost per sedan and compact shown in Exhibit 1-1.1 throughout the CCC case. To minimize assembly, CCC contracts with its suppliers to deliver large subassemblies. The sedan requires 25 subassemblies and the compact 20.

Financial Information

Balance sheets and income statements for CCC are presented in Exhibit 1-1.2 for 1999 through 2001 (actual results) and 2002 (projected). Note that three zeros have been dropped from all numbers in the financial statements, but not the computations below. For example, planned cash at the end of year 2002 is $1,462,000, not $1,462. The purpose for doing this is

---

[1] NUMMI is short for the New United Motor Manufacturing, Inc., a joint venture of Toyota and General Motors.

to make the statements easier to read. Financial statements for actual companies normally drop zeros. Ford Motor Company, for instance, drops six zeros from all dollar amounts in its financial statements. Note that CCC has been experiencing rapid growth and expects that to continue in 2002.

Exhibit 1-1.1
California Car Company
Bill of Materials

Part Code	Part Name	Chassis Assembly	Final Assembly	Cost of Each	Total Cost
Sedan					
811 Y	Batteries	2	0	$ 96	$ 192
943 B	Body base	1	0	324	324
720 B	Front wheel assembly	2	0	76	152
730 B	Rear wheel assembly	2	0	102	204
642 R	Floor panels	4	0	66	264
428 R	Axle Mounts	4	0	21	84
Chassis Assembly Total					$ 1,220
111 R	Taillight	0	1	$ 24	$ 24
214 R	Headlight	0	1	40	40
232 Y	Motor/Hood	0	2	573	1,146
212 Y	Windows	0	4	95	380
219 R	Roof panel	0	2	85	170
Final Assembly Total		—	—		$ 1,760
Sedan Totals		15	10		$ 2,980
Compact					
201 R	Axle Mounts	4	0	$ 21	$ 84
811 Y	Battery	1	0	96	96
943 B	Body base	1	0	214	214
720 B	Front wheel assembly	2	0	76	152
730 B	Rear wheel assembly	2	0	102	204
Chassis Assembly Total					$ 750
111 R	Taillight	0	1	$ 24	$ 24
214 R	Headlight	0	1	40	40
212 Y	Windows	0	2	95	190
422 R	Motor	0	2	480	960
421 R	Rear panel	0	2	85	170
440 Y	Solar panel, small	0	1	418	418
441 R	Solar panel, large	0	1	808	808
Final Assembly Total		—	—		$ 2,610
Compact Totals		10	10		$ 3,360

Each Part is described by an alphanumeric code:
   The first three digits are a unique part code
   The last digit is the part color code (black, red, or yellow)

Exhibit 1-1.2

California Car Company
Financial Statements
(In Thousands of Dollars)

BALANCE SHEETS	Planned 2002	Actual 2001	Actual 2000	Actual 1999
Assets				
Cash	$ 1,462	$ 350	$ 400	$ 250
Accounts receivable—net	13,600	1,450	435	160
Direct material inventory	1,590	618	95	17
Work-in-process inventory	3,267	250	16	6
Finished goods inventory	2,238	2,238	111	111
Total current assets	22,157	4,906	1,057	544
Long-term assets—net	112,000	42,000	5,560	4,000
Total assets	$ 134,157	$ 46,906	$ 6,617	$ 4,544
Total liabilities	$ 44,868	$ 23,707	$ 819	$ 171
Shareholders' equity				
Contributed capital	80,000	22,000	7,000	5,750
Retained earnings	9,289	1,199	(1,202)	(1,377)
Total shareholders' equity	89,289	23,199	5,798	4,373
Total liabilities and shareholders' equity	$ 134,157	$ 46,906	$ 6,617	$ 4,544

INCOME STATEMENTS	Planned 2002	Actual 2001	Actual 2000	Actual 1999
Sales revenue*	$ 136,000	$ 31,800	$ 9,500	$ 1,600
Less: cost of goods sold	98,943	20,670	6,650	1,109
Gross margin	37,057	11,130	2,850	491
Less: Selling expenses	7,000	1,500	600	400
Administrative expenses	18,500	6,200	2,000	1,200
Income before tax	11,557	3,430	250	(1,109)
Less: income tax—30%	3,467	1,029	75	(333)
Net income	$ 8,090	$ 2,401	$ 175	$ (776)

*Sedan unit sales	5,100	900	225	100
Sedan selling price	21,000			
Total sedan sales	$ 107,100,000			
Compact unit sales	1,700	300	75	0
Compact selling price	17,000			
Total compact sales	$ 28,900,000			
Total CCC sales	$ 136,000,000			

Serial Cases

The California Car Company is a serial case that extends over a period of four years, as the timeline in Exhibit 1-1.3 shows. A serial case involves a sequence of decisions related to a single company over a period of time. During this course you will follow CCC as it progresses from a rather small automobile assembly firm to a sophisticated, global corporation. The rationale for using a serial case is that students should more fully understand and appreciate the processes and integrated nature of business if they follow one company through many decision situations. To maximize the learning experience, students must keep current with their case assignments and understand the progression and timing of CCC's decisions. You should, therefore, refer back to Exhibit 1-1.3 periodically during the course to better understand how each individual case relates to others.

Exhibit 1-1.3
California Car Company Timeline

Date	Case	Topic
Year 2001		
November:	Cases 1-1, 1-2, 1-3	Introduction to CCC
December:	Case 1-4	Estimating Manufacturing Costs
Year 2002		
March:	Case 1-5	Pricing and Profitability
March:	Case 1-6	Job-Order Costing
April:	Case 1-7	Performance Variances
May:	Case 2-1	Activity-Based Budgeting
June:	Case 2-2	Implementing a Quality Program
June:	Case 2-3, Part I	Cost of Quality
August:	Case 2-4	Implementing JIT
September:	Case 2-5	JIT Costing
November:	Cases 3-1, 3-2, 3-4	Budgeting
November:	Case 3-6	Opening a Foreign Subsidiary
Year 2003		
February:	Case 2-3, Part II	Cost of Quality
July:	Case 3-3	Ethical Decision
October:	Case 3-5	Balanced Scorecard

Requirements

1. What specific products does CCC manufacture?

2. Why is the demand for CCC's products increasing so fast?

3. List the production departments through which CCC's products pass. In other words, which departments work directly on making cars or parts for the cars and thus add direct materials or direct labor to the cars? What are CCC's manufacturing overhead departments?

4. Are CCC's organizational structure and plant layout typical for a manufacturing organization? Answer this question the best you can based on your work experience and the course work you have completed.

5. What is the difference between product costs and period costs? List those CCC costs that are considered to be period costs. What are the three broad cost categories that comprise product costs at CCC? What cost categories at CCC can be included in inventory?

6. What are the three types of inventory in CCC's factory?

7. Based on the financial statements in Exhibit 1-1.2, what is CCC's total planned manufacturing costs for 2002?

8. Compute the following four ratios for CCC for both 2001 and 2002:

   - Return on equity

   - Return on sales

   - Inventory turnover

   - Debt-to-equity

9. Compute CCC's projected return-on-equity ratio for 2003 assuming that the income statement and balance sheet for 2003 are identical to those shown for 2002. Why is the 2003 return on equity so much lower than in 2002?

10. Average ratios for the hybrid car industry are as follows:

    - Return on equity   .212

    - Return on sales   .065

    - Inventory turnover   20.400

    - Debt-to-equity   1.450

    Discuss CCC's performance compared to the industry average performance. Identify two actions CCC could take that would improve its return on equity.

11. What is a serial case? Why is a serial case used in this course?

12. Your instructor will arrange for you to be given the title of one of CCC's four senior managers: (1) president, (2) vice president of production, (3) vice president of marketing, or (4) vice president of finance.

    a. Describe the typical educational background and business experience of a manager with your title.

    b. What primary decision(s) would a manager with your title address? Explain.

Case 1-2

CALIFORNIA CAR COMPANY
PRODUCTION LINE SIMULATION

Case Objectives

1. Introduce students to basic production concepts in a traditional plant setting
2. Demonstrate the linkage of cost accounting numbers to the operations of a firm

INTRODUCTION

To gain an understanding of the relationship between a physical production process and related cost information, you will participate in an in-class simulation of CCC's production process. CCC uses the same production process to produce both its sedan and compact models. CCC employs a traditional, departmentalized production layout. Activities in the plant are grouped by the type of work done. For example, all chassis assembly is done in the Chassis Assembly Department and all maintenance employees work in the Maintenance Department. Sedans and compacts pass through both production departments in batches. All overhead support is drawn from specialized overhead departments. Extensive setups are required on the equipment in the production departments to switch models. CCC believes that by specializing in a specific function, overall efficiency will be increased because all employees will be experts in their areas.

On the day of the simulation, small groups will be organized into independent production lines that mirror CCC's plant layout shown in Exhibit I-2 in the case introduction. Two small groups normally will team up to form a production line. A simplified schematic showing the production flow for the simulation is presented as Exhibit 1-2.1. Each student will act out an assigned role during the simulation.

You will produce cars in lots of 5 compacts and 15 sedans. A lot is the number of units of one product that is manufactured before the equipment is switched over to make another product. The 15 sedans will be manufactured in batches of 5. Batch size is the number of units within a lot that are manufactured and moved through the plant at once. For the compact, lot size and batch size are the same. *For the sedan, however, the lot size is 15, but the batch size is only 5.*

A key measure in traditional manufacturing operations is the number of units produced. Similarly, the primary measure of your production line's performance is the number of cars produced. Therefore, the production line that produces the most *defect-free* units in a set period of time will be deemed the winner. A production line is disqualified from the competition if any one of its members violates the rules of the simulation.

Important Note

Some schools may be using sets of toy blocks that are different than those shown in this book. If so, your instructor will provide you with drawings of your set of blocks to replace Exhibit 1-2.2, a new bill of materials to replace Exhibit 1-1.1, and a new set of assembly instructions to replace Exhibit 1-2.3.

Exhibit 1-2.1

Schematic of Traditional Simulation Layout
(Arrows Show the Flow of Parts and Cars)

| Chassis Assembly | → | Work-In-Process Inventory | → | Final Assembly | → | Inspection | → | Finished Goods Inventory |

Setup Jigs

Customer

Chassis Assembly Parts   Final Assembly Parts

STUDENT ROLES IN THE PRODUCTION PROCESS

Students will be assigned one of ten different roles in the simulation. It is important that you study the responsibilities of your assigned role carefully so that your group can compete effectively against other groups. The simulation roles are listed below.

1. Setup person
2. Chassis material handler
3. Chassis assembler
4. Final assembly material handler
5. Final assembler

6. Inspector
7. Accountant
8. Plant manager
9. Customer
10. Union steward

Setup Person

A setup person puts in place the proper tooling jig for the assembly of a chassis in the Chassis Assembly Department or completion of a car in the Final Assembly Department. A jig is an apparatus used to help hold or align parts during assembly. Time and motion studies at the design stage prior to production have shown that utilizing a jig is the most cost-effective method of assembly.

Exhibit 1-2.2
California Car Company
Sedan and Compact Car Design

SEDAN

Chassis Assembly

1) Underneath and at each end of the black body panel, attach one large red panel.
2) Attach two large red panels side by side across the top of the black body panel, placing them one peg away from the edge. Repeat at other end.
3) Center and attach two wheels under each pair of red panels.
4) Attach one red panel crosswise between each set of wheels to complete each axle.
5) Place the two large yellow "batteries" under the body panel between the axles.

Front   Back

Completed Chassis

SEDAN

Final Assembly

1) Attach one large red panel on top of each inner large red panel already attached to the black body panel.
2) Attach one small red piece on top of the black body panel at each end.
3) Attach two flat yellow "hood" panels on the front large red panel.
4) Attach two windows on each inner large red panel.
5) Attach two large red panels to the top of each set of windows.

Front   Back

Completed Sedan

COMPACT

Chassis Assembly
1) Center the yellow "battery" under the black body panel.
2) Attach the four wheels under the black body panel placing them next to the yellow "battery".
3) Attach two small red mounts crosswise under each set of wheel "axles" to hold the wheels on.

Front

Back

Completed Chassis

COMPACT

Final Assembly

1) Stack two red panels and attach on top of the black body base placing them one peg in from the end. Repeat on the other end.
2) Attach one small red piece at each end of body base.
3) Attach the small yellow "solar panel/hood" on the front set of red panels.
4) Attach one window on each set of red panels.
5) Attach a large red "solar panel/roof" to the top of the windows.

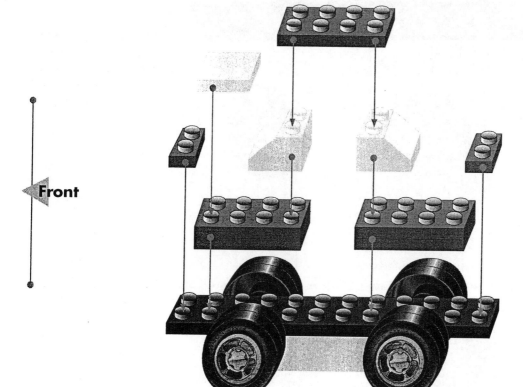

Front   Back

Completed Compact

Special Instructions

For purposes of the simulation, your instructor will provide the items to represent the jigs. These may be wooden devices or simply cardboard templates that need to be changed. Remember, however, that in a real factory changing jigs can be both difficult and time consuming. The chassis and final assemblers will call you for a setup when they are finished producing a lot. Your instructor also may tell you the minimum setup time to use. If so, it is your job to ensure that the assemblers do not begin work until the full setup time has expired. You should wait at a desk away from the assembly line until an assembler calls for a setup.

Chassis Material Handler

This person, when notified by the chassis assembler, selects parts from inventory storage bins and delivers a pallet of parts that contains sufficient quantities of each part to produce *five* chassis. A pallet is represented by a paper cup or some other container, into which the necessary parts are placed. You can place all parts for one batch in one cup. Use the bill of materials (Exhibit 1-1.1) and the drawings (Exhibit 1-2.2) to identify the parts used to assemble sedan and compact chassis. Just deliver the pallet (cup) of parts to the assembler, and the assembler will handle them from there. It is critical that you learn the parts you will deliver *before the simulation*, because slow delivery of parts will reduce the output of the entire line. The chassis assembler will begin the simulation by producing 15 sedans, 5 at a time.

Special Instructions

1. You are not allowed to fill cups from inventory before the assembler calls for parts.

2. The assembler cannot call for parts, and you are not allowed to retrieve parts, until that person begins assembling the last chassis in the batch.

3. If you grab or are given a defective part (wrong color) by your instructor, you must deliver it. You *cannot* exchange it for a correctly colored part.

4. If you deliver too few parts, you must make a special delivery of the missing parts before you deliver the next batch of parts.

5. If you deliver too many parts, you must retrieve those parts, plus you must wait 30 seconds before you deliver the parts for the next batch.

Chassis Assembler

Using the tooling jig for the appropriate vehicle, a chassis assembler assembles an individual chassis. The steps for chassis assembly of a sedan and a compact are listed in Exhibit 1-2.3. It is critical that you learn how to assemble the parts before the simulation, because slow assembly of parts will reduce the output of the entire line. It is your job to call for a setup at the completion of each lot and to tell the material handler to get parts when you are assembling the last chassis in a batch. *You will begin the simulation by assembling a lot of 15 sedan chassis, 5 at a time*. You will then assemble 5 compact chassis, followed by 15 sedan chassis, and so forth.

Upon completion of a batch, at CCC or at a real-life manufacturer, the assembler would call for a chassis material handler to move the assembled chassis to work-in-process (WIP) storage located between Buildings 1 and 2. In our in-class simulation, instead of relying on the material handler to move the completed chassis to the WIP area, the assembler will move the chassis. *You may not move any chassis to the WIP area until the full batch of five cars is complete.*

Exhibit 1-2.3
Step-By-Step Assembly Instructions

Sedan
Chassis Assembly
1. Underneath and at each end of the black body base, attach one large red panel.
2. Attach two large red panels side by side across the top of the black body panel, placing them one peg from the end. Repeat at the other end.
3. Center and attach two wheels under each pair of red panels.
4. Attach one large red panel crosswise between each set of wheels to complete each axle.
5. Place two large yellow "batteries" under the body base between the axles.

Final Assembly
1. Attach one large red panel on top of each inner large red panel already attached to the black body panel.
2. Attach one small red piece on top of the black body panel at each end.
3. Attach two flat yellow "hood" panels on the front large red panel.
4. Attach two windows on each inner large red panel.
5. Attach two large red panels to the top of each set of windows.

Compact
Chassis Assembly
1. Center the yellow "battery" under the black body panel.
2. Attach the four wheels under the black body panel placing them next to the yellow "battery."
3. Attach the two small red mounts crosswise under each set of wheel "axles" to hold the wheels on.

Final Assembly
1. Stack two red flat panels and attach them to the top of the black body base, placing them one peg in from the end. Repeat on the other end.
2. Attach one small red piece at each end of the body base.
3. Attach the small yellow "solar panel/hood" on the front set of red panels.
4. Attach one window on each set of red panels.
5. Attach the large red "solar panel/roof" to the top of the windows.

Special Instructions

1. You cannot call for more parts until you have started assembling the last car in a batch.
2. You cannot call for a setup until you have finished the current lot of 15 sedans or 5 compacts.
3. You must assemble defective (wrong colored) parts, even if you have extra good parts.

4. If the material handler delivers too many or too few parts, you must call the handler back to correct the situation before bringing parts for the next batch.

5. On a separate sheet of paper, keep track of the approximate amount of time you are idle while waiting for parts and setups.

Information You Must Collect for the Accountant

At the end of the simulation, estimate the percent of time you were idle while waiting for parts or setups. Record that percentage on Exhibit 1-2.4, item 8. The accountant will ask for this at the end of the simulation.

Final Assembly Material Handler

This person, when notified by the final assembler, selects parts from inventory storage bins and delivers a pallet of parts that contains sufficient quantities of each part to produce *five* completed vehicles. A pallet is represented by a paper cup or some other container, into which the necessary parts are placed. You can place all parts for one batch in one cup. Use the bill of materials (Exhibit 1-1.1) and the drawings (Exhibit 1-2.2) to identify the parts used in the final assembly of sedans and compacts. Just deliver the pallet (cup) of parts to the assembler, and the assembler will handle them from there. It is critical that you learn the parts you will deliver *before the simulation*, because slow delivery of parts will reduce the output of the entire line. When asked by the final assembler, you also move batches of five chassis from the WIP inventory to the final assembler. The final assembler will begin the simulation by performing final assembly on five compacts.

Special Instructions

1. You are not allowed to fill cups from inventory before the assembler calls for parts.

2. The assembler cannot call for parts until that person begins final assembly of the last car in the batch.

3. If you grab or are given a defective part (wrong color) by your instructor, you must deliver it. You cannot exchange it for a correctly colored part.

4. If you deliver too few parts, you must make a special delivery of the missing parts before you deliver the next batch of parts.

5. If you deliver too many parts, you must retrieve those parts, plus you must wait 30 seconds before you deliver the parts for the next batch.

Final Assembler

Using the tooling jig for the appropriate vehicle, a final assembler assembles an individual vehicle. The steps for the final assembly of a sedan and a compact are listed in Exhibit 1-2.3. It is critical that you learn how to assemble the parts *before the simulation*, because slow assembly of parts will reduce the output of the entire line. It is your job to call for a setup at the completion of each lot and to tell the material handler to get parts when you are assembling the last car in a batch. You also must tell the material handler to deliver a batch of five chassis from the WIP inventory (if five chassis are in inventory). When you have completed a batch of five cars, you can move them to the inspection area. *You will begin the simulation by finishing the assembly of five compacts*. You will then finish the assembly of 15 sedans, followed by 5 compacts, and so forth.

Special Instructions

1. You cannot call for more parts and chassis from work-in-process until you have started assembling the last car in a batch of five.

2. You cannot call for a setup until you have finished the current lot of 5 compacts or 15 sedans.

3. You must assemble defective (wrong colored) parts, even if you have extra good parts.

4. If the material handler delivers too many or too few parts, you must call the handler back to correct the situation before bringing parts for the next batch.

5. On a separate sheet of paper, keep track of the approximate time you are idle while waiting for parts and setups.

Information You Must Collect for the Accountant

At the end of the simulation, estimate the percent of time you were idle while waiting for parts or setups. Record that percentage on Exhibit 1-2.4, item 8. The accountant will ask for this at the end of the simulation.

Inspector

This person performs thorough inspections and parks each good vehicle in the finished goods storage area. Cars that do not pass final inspection are appropriately marked and are set aside for rework at a later time. Inspect the cars carefully. Wrong color parts, improper assembly, and poor fit are considered defects. The timing marker the accountant has attached to a car is not a defect. The inspector will be selected from another production line so that the inspector will have an incentive to perform a rigorous inspection.

Information You Must Collect for the Accountant

At the end of the simulation, count the number of defective cars. Record the number on Exhibit 1-2.4, item 5, and give that number to the accountant when asked.

Customer

The customer draws a playing card or some other sales marker at a fixed time interval determined by your instructor. If you use playing cards, a club represents a compact sale, and spades, hearts, and diamonds represent sedan sales. The customer removes the model indicated from finished goods inventory and places the car in a separate sold-car area. The card is then placed in the sold car stack. If a card is drawn and that model is not in finished goods inventory at the moment the card is drawn, then your line has a stockout. Place the card in a stockout pile that is separate from the sold-car pile. Once a stockout occurs the sale is lost forever. That is, the customer *does not* convert a stockout to a sale as soon as that model is available again.

You draw a card as soon as the instructor tells your group to start the simulation. At the end of the simulation, the number of cars placed in the sold-car area plus the number of stockouts should reconcile with the number of playing cards you have drawn. For example, if your instructor tells you to run the simulation for 15 minutes with sales occurring every 30 seconds, the total number of sold cars plus stockouts should equal 30. *You will need a watch or clock that indicates seconds to perform your role.*

Information You Must Collect for the Accountant

At the end of the simulation, you record the number of units sold and the total number of stockouts *by model* on Exhibit 1-2.4, items 2 and 3, respectively, and give this information to the accountant when asked.

Accountant

During the simulation the accountant is responsible for collecting the cycle time measurement. This is done by first marking any sedan chassis in the third batch of 5 sedans in the first lot of 15 sedan chassis produced and recording the time at which chassis assembly began. You then watch the marked chassis and record the time it takes for it to arrive in finished goods inventory (not in the sold-car area). Cycle time is the difference in the recorded times.

After the simulation has ended, the accountant is required to do the following in order to complete Exhibit 1-2.4:

1. Record the number of sedans and compacts in work-in-process and finished goods ending inventories.

2. Collect from the customer the number of sedans sold and the number of sedan stockouts. Collect the same information for the compacts.

3. Collect from the inspector the number of defective units needing rework.

4. Collect from the chassis and final assemblers their idle time estimates.

5. Calculate good units completed for both sedans and compacts, which equal:

   Sales + Ending inventory finished goods – Beginning inventory finished goods.

6. Compute average production time per unit. Average production is obtained by determining the number of seconds the simulation ran and dividing that number by the total number of good units produced (sedan and compact combined). For example, if the simulation ran for 15 minutes and 25 good units were produced, you divide 900 seconds (15 minutes × 60 seconds) by 25 cars, for an average production time of 36 seconds per car.

7. Record the cycle time for the marked sedan.

Finally, it is the accountant's responsibility to ensure that all members of the groups working on the production line have copied all of the information from the accountant's completed Exhibit 1-2.4 onto their own form. All students will need a completed Exhibit 1-2.4 in order to finish Part II of Case 1-2.

Plant Manager

The plant manager supervises the entire operation and troubleshoots during any unforeseen difficulties. It is the plant manager's job to learn the responsibilities of each job and to provide advice on how to improve operations, as long as the advice does not violate simulation rules. Some instructors may assign the plant manager the task of breaking down sold cars and returning the parts to the part bins.

Union Steward

The union steward observes the operation of the entire line and makes sure that all procedures are being followed. If a violation of procedure is detected, the line shuts down for 30 seconds while the union steward explains the violation. The union steward must be familiar with all procedures discussed in this case. This person will be selected from another assembly line so that there will be an incentive to enforce the rules.

Part I Requirements (Perform Prior to the Simulation)

In order for the simulation to proceed smoothly during the class session, each student must complete the following advance preparation steps outside of class.

1. Meet briefly with other members of your production line and review the steps needed to assemble both the sedan and compact models. See Exhibit 1-2.2 or drawings provided by your instructor and Exhibit 1-2.3 for the step-by-step sequence involved in the assembly of each car. See Exhibit 1-1.1 for a bill of materials for each car. Since CCC evaluates production line performance based on the number of good cars completed in a set time, your goal in the simulation is to produce as many defect-free cars as possible while following all stated procedures.

2. Become familiar with the schematic for the simulation in Exhibit 1-2.1. In addition, understand the following terms:

    *   *Lot size*—the number of vehicles produced before a setup occurs. CCC's lot sizes are 15 sedans and 5 compacts,

    *   *Batch size*—the number of vehicles produced from one delivery of material. CCC's batch size is five cars, the same for sedans and compacts,

    *   *Production line*—the Chassis and Assembly Departments and all support services needed to produce completed cars. Your class probably will have multiple lines.

3. Become familiar with the roles and steps in CCC's production described in the case. Note that all steps are identical for each model, only the parts and time required to execute a step will differ depending on the model. Be sure to read and fully understand the instructions for your job.

Part II Requirements (Perform as Follow-Up to the Simulation)

Prepare a one-page, single-spaced, word-processed analysis of the simulation that provides the following:

1. A brief description of your tasks and how they relate to the tasks performed by others. Include a discussion of the following:

    a. How do your tasks affect the work done by others?

    b. How does the work performed by others affect your tasks?

    c. How much does your job add value to the car from the customers' perspective?

    d. Are the costs associated with your tasks direct or overhead costs? If they are overhead costs, how do accountants assign these costs to the cars?

2. A brief identification of any weaknesses/inefficiencies that you noticed involving your assigned tasks and the tasks that you observed being performed by others.

3. Complete the Accounting Data Sheet (Exhibit 1-2.4) and attach it to your answer. You will need to get much of the data from your group's accountant. Discuss why:

    a.   The cycle time was so much higher than the average time to produce a car.

    b.   The chassis and final assemblers were idle for as long as your accountant reported.

    c.   Your group had stockouts.

Exhibit 1-2.4
California Car Company
Accounting Data Sheet for a Traditional Plant Layout

Assembly Line Number _____

	Recorded Value		
	Sedan	Compact	
1. Inventory Levels:			
Beginning work-in-process	0	5	
Beginning finished goods	6	2	
Ending work-in-process			
Ending finished goods			
2. Sales			
3. Stockouts			
			CCC Total
4. Good Units Completed			=
5. Defective Units			
6. Cycle Time (Sedan Only)			

	Both Models Combined
7. Average Production Time	
8. Assembler Idle Time Percentage	

Group Assignment 1-2

ASSEMBLING CARS AT
CALIFORNIA CAR COMPANY

Group number _____   **Signatures of group members participating:**

_____

_____

Objectives

1. Introduce students to basic production concepts in a traditional plant setting
2. Demonstrate the linkage of cost accounting numbers to the operations of a firm
3. Familiarize students with the products and manufacturing processes of CCC

Requirements

Group Assignment 1-2 is a simulation of CCC's manufacturing process using a departmental production layout. Enter the required information below. You will receive credit for being prepared and actively participating. If anyone in your group did not prepare and/or did not actively participate, do not include that person's name above.

	Sedan	Compact
Total units sold	_____	_____
Total stockouts	_____	_____
Total good units completed	_____	_____
Defective units	_____	_____

Case 1-3

PRODUCTION PROBLEMS AT CALIFORNIA CAR COMPANY

Case Objectives

1. Reinforce production concepts developed in the simulation
2. Relate accounting costs to production activities

Decision: Is CCC's plant operating efficiently?

PROBLEMS EXPOSED BY THE SIMULATION

Sally Swanson, CCC's vice president of production, just viewed a production simulation video and was very interested to see that many features of the CCC production process were also evident in the video. Moreover, the video stimulated a number of questions in Sally's mind about the efficiency and effectiveness of CCC's assembly process. After circulating the video among her management group, Sally called a meeting of her plant manager, engineers, production line supervisors, and the head of inspection and raised the following questions:

1. "We (CCC) and the firm in the video both seem to keep adequate levels of raw materials and work-in-process inventories. Yet both companies experience frequent stockouts of finished products. Why does this happen? What do you think it really costs us to have a stockout of sedans or compacts?"

2. "In my walks around our plant, I frequently see workers who are idle. I noticed the same problem in the video. Why can't either company keep its workers busy throughout the workday? What does idle time really cost us? How can we reduce idle time?"

3. "Did you notice the disruption that occurred in the video when the template jig broke down at the second work station where the worker was drawing circles using the template jig? We frequently have breakdowns in our tooling that also cause disruptions. I wonder what these breakdowns are costing us. How can we avoid them?"

4. "I noticed that the firm in the video inspects its products just as we do at the end of its production process in order to prevent bad units from reaching the customer. Also, they seemed to have a defect problem just like we do. I wonder what defects are currently costing us. How can we reduce the defect problem?"

5. "Setups halted the production process in the video the same way they shut down our assembly line. I wonder whether we should increase the size of our production runs, say from 5 to 10 for compacts and possibly from 15 to 30 for our sedans, in order to reduce the number of setups. What costs per car do you think would change if we increased the size of our production runs?"

6. "As in the video, our cycle time is quite high. Many of our customers want 'special' extras such as sunroofs or built-in, high-quality sound systems, but they don't want to wait a long time for delivery. These specials are very profitable. How can we reduce our cycle time in order to attract more of this business?"

Requirements

For each of the above questions, write a one-paragraph word-processed response to Sally Swanson in which you present your interpretation and analysis of the problem that she has identified and your suggestions for addressing the problem.

Case 1-4

DEVELOPMENT OF PRODUCT COST
ESTIMATES FOR 2002

Case Objectives

1. Introduce the concept of predetermined overhead rates
2. Introduce product costing in a general way, using estimated costs for next year
3. Demonstrate the nature and flow of costs
4. Improve spreadsheet graphing skills

Decision (Planning): What costs of producing cars should be used in planning for 2002?

Note: In this case, CCC is preparing cost information for both planning and pricing purposes, which are addressed in more detail later in the course.

COST ESTIMATION

It is now December 2001, and you are assisting Mary Jones, head of accounting for CCC, in preparing manufacturing cost estimates for the company's sedan and compact vehicles. Mary needs product cost estimates in order to complete her preparation of projected financial statements for 2002. CCC plans to produce 5,100 sedans and 1,700 compacts in 2002. Mary explains: "I need you to figure out the amount of direct materials, direct labor, and manufacturing overhead that should be assigned to each car built next year based on our expected purchase costs, results of our recent labor wage negotiations, and expected overhead cost structure."

Direct Material and Direct Labor

Mary continues: "Direct materials for each car should be no problem. Our current bills of materials have been updated to reflect purchase prices that we expect to pay in 2002 for each part used in production." The bills of materials for sedan and compact models is presented in Exhibit 1-1.1. "Direct labor also is simple. Our production records show that it is presently taking about 108 hours of direct labor to produce a sedan, 52 hours in chassis assembly and 56 hours in final assembly. A compact requires 65 hours, 28 hours in chassis assembly and 37 hours in final assembly. We just completed negotiations for next year's wage and fringe package, and an average wage rate of $35 per direct labor hour will apply for 2002."

Manufacturing Overhead

Mary then tells you: "The development of overhead cost estimates for the sedan and compact, however, is not so simple. Our present cost system doesn't provide much detail on our overhead costs, and we don't yet have a good understanding of how overhead costs are influenced by changes in the ratio of sedans versus compacts produced each month."

"To get started on the overhead problem, let's take a look at this year's (2001) monthly data. Assume that overhead varies with the number of DLHs, so we can use direct labor as the measure of activity. Once we can come up with a reasonable formula for estimating total overhead for 2002, we can use that estimate to develop a predetermined overhead rate based on DLHs. That rate can then be used to assign a reasonable amount of estimated overhead to a sedan and to a compact. It is important for planning purposes, however, to develop the overhead rate in two components: fixed and variable."

Mary went back to her office and gathered all the overhead cost data for 2001 that she could find. She was able to develop data for variable manufacturing overhead for the first 10 months of 2001. Using the 10 months of variable manufacturing overhead data and discussions with production supervisors, Mary then estimated variable overhead for November and December. She presents you with a spreadsheet showing the total and variable overhead information she has developed (Exhibit 1-4.1).

Exhibit 1-4.1
California Car Company
Overhead Costs for 2001

Month	Direct Labor Hours	Manufacturing Overhead Total	Variable
January	3,475	$ 507,263	$ 137,263
February	3,265	497,335	127,335
March	4,430	542,770	172,770
April	5,400	577,900	207,900
May	8,470	683,390	313,390
June	7,920	667,000	297,000
July	8,910	696,106	326,106
August	9,360	706,960	336,960
September	9,900	726,400	356,400
October	13,180	818,120	448,120
November (Est.)	12,960	813,880	443,880
December (Est.)	12,730	802,876	432,876
Totals for 2001	**100,000**	**$ 8,040,000**	**$ 3,600,000**

Finally, Mary tells you: "Since we will not change the way we manufacture cars, and variable costs per unit remain constant as volume changes, the variable overhead rate per DLH should be about the same in 2002 as in 2001. Therefore, *you can get an estimated variable overhead rate for 2002 by taking the total variable overhead for 2001 (as shown in Exhibit 1-4.1) and dividing it by total DLHs for 2001.* Then you multiply this variable overhead rate by the total estimated DLHs for 2002 to get total estimated variable manufacturing overhead for the year 2002.

"With our major expansion this coming year, and with adding another building area for production, we have accumulated a large amount of fixed production costs. We have to incorporate these new fixed costs, as well as our variable overhead costs, into our manufacturing overhead cost estimates for the coming year. Therefore, we *cannot* use last year's actual fixed overhead as an estimate for this year." With the help of the production managers, Mary was able to determine that *fixed overhead* associated with production in 2002 is expected to total about $31,081,100.

You think to yourself, "What?" Luckily, you have written down exactly what Mary has said, so you go back to your office and attempt to develop formula relationships from her verbal instructions.

Requirements

Set up a computer spreadsheet in the format of Exhibit 1-4.2 to organize your work and to make the required calculations. Be sure to use formulas and cell references wherever possible so "what if" questions are easily answered. It is particularly important to use cell formulas in computing the predetermined variable and fixed overhead rates.

1. Develop a year 2002 estimate for direct labor for each car model assuming that (a) a sedan and compact require 108 and 65 hours of direct labor, respectively; and (b) direct labor employees will be paid $35 per hour. In other words, complete the outlined cells for three direct labor rows in Exhibit 1-4.2: Direct labor cost—sedan (cells C20–F20); Direct labor cost—compact (cells C29–F29); and Direct labor cost—total (cells D38–F38).

2. Determine if the data in Exhibit 1-4.1 indicate that DLHs is a good choice for a variable overhead activity measure. Use your spreadsheet software to graph the direct labor hour–variable overhead cost relationship. Instructions for using the Chart function in Excel are presented at the end of this case. In your chart, illustrate the relationship between DLHs and variable overhead and total overhead. Put DLH on the horizontal or X-axis and overhead costs on the vertical or Y-axis.

3. Regardless of your answer to requirement 2, assume that CCC allocates overhead on the basis of DLHs. Estimate the 2002 plantwide predetermined *variable* manufacturing overhead rate per hour based on the 2001 data presented in Exhibit 1-4.1. Enter your variable overhead estimate in the "Predetermined variable OH rate" cell (D13) on your spreadsheet. Then complete all three rows with a "Variable manufacturing overhead" label.

4. Enter the predetermined *fixed* manufacturing overhead in the "Predetermined fixed OH rate" cell (D14) on your spreadsheet. Estimate the plantwide predetermined fixed overhead rate per hour by using the formula below. The denominator must be entered by cell references only.

$$\text{Predetermined Fixed overhead rate} = \frac{\text{Total estimated fixed overhead ($31,081,100)}}{\text{Total 2002 estimated direct labor hours}}$$

The total estimated direct labor hours for 2002 is found in Exhibit 1-4.1. You can now complete your spreadsheet by completing all three rows with a "Fixed manufacturing overhead" label and the three "Total" rows. At this point all of the blank cells in Exhibit 1-4.2 should be filled in. If your spreadsheet is missing has any blank cells, complete them now. Turn in a printout of your spreadsheet at this point and the spreadsheet formulas.

5. Sally Swanson believes that with some hard work and creative problem solving, the number of hours required to manufacture a sedan can be reduced to 103 DLHs in year 2002 instead of the 108 used in your estimates. The entire five-hour reduction would occur in final assembly. Prepare a new estimated 2002 product cost spreadsheet for CCC using 103 DLHs per sedan. Print out your new solution.

Exhibit 1-4.2
California Car Company
Estimated 2002 Product Costs

	A	B	C	D	E	F
5				Per Unit		
6				Chassis	Final	Total
7				Assembly	Assembly	
8	Direct materials—sedan			$ 1,220	$ 1,760	$ 2,980
9	Direct labor hours—sedan			52	56	108
10	Direct materials—compact			$ 750	$ 2,610	$ 3,360
11	Direct labor hours—compact			28	37	65
12	Direct labor wage rate =			$ 35.00		
13	Predetermined variable OH rate =					
14	Predetermined fixed OH rate =				(Use cell references for DLH)	
15				TOTAL COSTS		
16	**Sedan costs:**		Per	Chassis	Final	Total
17	Units produced:	5,100	Sedan	Assembly	Assembly	Sedan
18	Direct labor hours		108	265,200	285,600	550,800
19	Direct material		$ 2,980	$ 6,222,000	$ 8,976,000	$ 15,198,000
20	Direct labor cost					
21	Variable manufacturing overhead					
22	Fixed manufacturing overhead					
23	Total sedan costs					
24						
25	**Compact costs:**		Per	Chassis	Final	Total
26	Units produced:	1,700	Compact	Assembly	Assembly	Compact
27	Direct labor hours		65	47,600	62,900	110,500
28	Direct material		$ 3,360	$ 1,275,000	$ 4,437,000	$ 5,712,000
29	Direct labor cost					
30	Variable manufacturing overhead					
31	Fixed manufacturing overhead					
32	Total compact costs					
33						
34	**CCC Totals:**			Chassis	Final	CCC
35				Assembly	Assembly	Totals
36	Direct labor hours			312,800	348,500	661,300
37	Direct material			$ 7,497,000	$ 13,413,000	$ 20,910,000
38	Direct labor cost					
39	Variable manufacturing overhead					
40	Fixed manufacturing overhead					
41	Total manufacturing costs					

Handwritten notes in margin: 5,525,300 and 200,00

6. Explain why the cost per compact changes in Requirement 5 when the estimated DLHs to manufacture a sedan decreases.

7. George Olson believes that CCC can sell only 4,800 sedans instead of the 5,100 in the original cost estimate spreadsheet. For this question, assume that the estimated DLHs to manufacture a sedan are back to 108 hours. Prepare a new estimated 2002 product cost spreadsheet for CCC using a production level of 4,800 sedans instead of 5,100 sedans, with production of the compacts remaining the same. Print out your answer. Put 5,100 back in the sedan production cell.

8. Explain why the cost per compact changes in Requirement 7 when the estimated number of sedans sold decreases.

9. After reviewing the cost estimates, Sally Swanson, CCC's vice president of production, remarked: "Discussing all the costs mentioned above got me thinking about how we assign overhead costs to products. Currently, we assign overhead based on the direct labor hours used to produce a model. The sedan takes more than 1.5 times the direct labor hours to manufacture, so it is assigned 1.5 times the overhead cost. It appears to me, however, that some overhead costs such as the idle time due to setups or the time required to inspect and perform rework are about the same regardless of the model produced. Do you think our cost accounting system is accurately costing our cars?"

EXCEL CHART (GRAPH) INSTRUCTIONS

Spreadsheet graphical tools are powerful and effective ways to present numerical information. This case requires you to graph the relationship between manufacturing overhead costs and direct labor hours. In Excel spreadsheet software, graphing is done using the Chart function. The following are instructions for using the Excel Chart function on Case 1-4 data.

1. Create and save a spreadsheet with the DLHs and overhead cost data in Exhibit 1-4.1.

   a. Enter column headings in row 1 (e.g., enter direct labor hours in cell A1).

   b. Enter the direct labor hours, the X-axis data, in column A and overhead dollar amounts in columns B and C, formatting DLHs for commas (,) and costs for dollars ($).

2. Highlight the entire data area in columns A, B, and C, including the first row with column headings.

3. Select "Insert" from the top menu bar, and then go to the down arrow.

4. Select "Chart" from the pull-down menu.

5. Select "XY Scatter" on the next screen.

6. Select "Next" at the bottom of the next screen

7. Select "Series in: Columns" on the next screen (this should be the default setting).

8. Select "Next" at the bottom of the screen.

9. Type in titles for chart and axes.

(Chart instructions continued on the next page)

10. Select "Next" at the bottom of the screen.

11. Select "As Object in: Sheet 1" (or whatever you have named your sheet).

12. Select "Finish" at the bottom of the screen.

13. To have some fun customizing the graph, double click on any of the following areas:

    a.   Axes numbers and titles (you probably will want to reduce the font size).

    b.   The chart area (white area outside of plot and other writing).

    c.   The plot area (colored area where the graph is).

    d.   Experiment with "Borders, Area Colors, Fill Effects, Fonts, and Alignment."

    e.   Click outside the chart area to delete the chart menu and return to the spreadsheet.

14. To print the graph, click on the graph area (you may want to remove the color background from the plot area first if you are printing in black and white).

    a.   Select "File" from the top menu bar.

    b.   Select "Page Setup" from the pull-down menu.

    c.   Select "Chart" from the next pull-down menu.

    d.   Select "Scale to Fit Page."

    e.   Select "Print Preview" to view the graph as it will be printed or to change the format of the graph.

    f.   Select "Print" from the pull-down menu.

    g.   Select "OK" to print.

    h.   *Note*: Some printers will not print a chart formatted in color.

Case 1-5

PROFITABILITY ISSUES AT
CALIFORNIA CAR COMPANY

Case Objectives

1. Introduce students to pricing decisions
2. Demonstrate the use of cost accounting information to support pricing decisions
3. Assess profitability of products and firms using financial data

Decision (Pricing): Does CCC need to adjust prices or reduce costs to remain competitive?

ASSESSING YEAR 2002 PRICES

It is now early March 2002. Jena Butler, Vice President of Finance, Sally Swanson, Vice President of Production, and George Olson, Vice President of Marketing, are presently working together on a project involving a review of the company's selling prices for its sedan and compact vehicles, which are currently set at $21,000 and $17,000, respectively. Up to now, the company has relied heavily on its assessment of customers' willingness to buy electric vehicles and on legal and political constraints in setting its prices. The project team believes that it should reexamine its current prices in light of recent industry data that the team has just received (see Exhibit 1-5.1). Jena also has compiled recent cost and budget information provided by the company's accounting system (see Exhibits 1-5.2 and 1-5.3, Case 1-4, and your individual solution to Case 1-4).

Exhibit 1-5.1
2001 Hybrid Vehicle Industry Percentage Income Statement

		Percent
Sales		100%
Cost of goods sold		
Direct materials	16%	
Direct labor	15%	
Manufacturing overhead	27%	
Total cost of goods sold		58%
Gross margin		42%
Selling and administrative expenses		
Selling expenses	10%	
Administrative expenses	19%	29%
Income before tax		13%
Income tax (30%)		4%
Net income		9%
Average industry sedan price		$ 20,000
Average industry compact price		$ 17,000

"Looking back, we've kept our prices constant at their current levels since 2000, and our budget for 2002 reflects those same prices," stated George. "I'm concerned that our prices are too high. If I'm right, we will miss both our 2002 sales volume targets and our profit targets. Our dealers tell me that they are losing sales to interested customers due to our prices. Can we be competitive in the long run by using our current prices? Let's reduce our profit on each car and cut the price of the sedan to $20,000 and the compact to $16,000. I wonder what our competitors are doing?" queried George.

"That's a good question," Sally responded. "When I look at our current prices in light of our estimated total manufacturing costs for 2002, those prices seem somewhat high. If our prices are too high, I'm worried about customers not buying our planned sales volume and the possibility of an inventory buildup during 2002 if they don't. However, we don't want to reduce our projected net income. Both our shareholders and creditors are demanding that level of profitability."

"I think you've both identified significant issues," said Jena. "I am concerned about the impact of a price reduction on our margins. Let me work up an analysis of the markups implied in our 2002 budget plan and a comparison of those markups with the competition. Let's plan to reconvene next Monday and go over the figures."

Exhibit 1-5.2
CCC Pricing and Cost Information
Based on 2002 Estimates in Case 1-4

		Sedan		Compact
Sales price		$ 21,000		$ 17,000
Direct materials cost		$ 2,980		$ 3,360
Direct labor cost		3,780		2,275
Manufacturing overhead:				
Variable	$ 3,888		$ 2,340	
Fixed	5,076	8,964	3,055	5,395
Total manufacturing cost		$ 15,724		$ 11,030
Production volume (in units)		5,100		1,700

Requirements

1. Complete the costs in the table below. Assume that $2,000,000 of selling expenses and $1,000,000 of administrative expenses are variable. Fixed manufacturing costs are inserted in the table. Add the variable costs. Leave the shaded cells blank.

	One Sedan	One Compact	All Sedans	All Compacts	CCC Total
Variable manufacturing costs					
Fixed manufacturing costs	$ 5,076	$ 3,055	$ 25,887,600	$ 5,193,500	$ 31,081,100
Total manufacturing costs					
Total variable costs					

Exhibit 1-5.3

California Car Company
Financial Statements
(In Thousands of Dollars)

BALANCE SHEETS	Planned 2002	Actual 2001	Actual 2000	Actual 1999
Assets				
Cash	$ 1,462	$ 350	$ 400	$ 250
Accounts receivable—net	13,600	1,450	435	160
Direct material inventory	1,590	618	95	17
Work-in-process inventory	3,267	250	16	6
Finished goods inventory	2,238	2,238	111	111
Total current assets	22,157	4,906	1,057	544
Long-term assets—net	112,000	42,000	5,560	4,000
Total assets	$ 134,157	$ 46,906	$ 6,617	$ 4,544
Total liabilities	$ 44,868	$ 23,707	$ 819	$ 171
Shareholders' equity				
Contributed capital	80,000	22,000	7,000	5,750
Retained earnings	9,289	1,199	(1,202)	(1,377)
Total shareholders' equity	89,289	23,199	5,798	4,373
Total liabilities and shareholders' equity	$ 134,157	$ 46,906	$ 6,617	$ 4,544

INCOME STATEMENTS	Planned 2002	Actual 2001	Actual 2000	Actual 1999
Sales revenue	$ 136,000	$ 31,800	$ 9,500	$ 1,600
Less: cost of goods sold	98,943	20,670	6,650	1,109
Gross margin	37,057	11,130	2,850	491
Less: Selling expenses	7,000	1,500	600	400
Administrative expenses	18,500	6,200	2,000	1,200
Income before tax	11,557	3,430	250	(1,109)
Less: income tax—30%	3,467	1,029	75	(333)
Net income	$ 8,090	$ 2,401	$ 175	$ (776)

2. In response to George's and Sally's concerns, determine the following:

   a. CCC's estimated year 2002 markup percentages on estimated *variable manufacturing cost per unit* for each type of vehicle, sedan and compact. You need to calculate two separate markup percentages.

   b. CCC's estimated year 2002 markup percentage on estimated *total manufacturing cost per unit* for each type of vehicle, sedan and compact. You need to calculate two separate markup percentages.

(The requirements are continued on the next page)

c. CCC's total year 2002 corporate markup percentage on estimated *total manufacturing costs* reflected in its 2002 budgeted income statement in Exhibit 1-5.3. You need to calculate only one separate markup percentage for all of CCC.

d. The industry average markup percentage in 2001 on *total manufacturing cost*. Use Exhibit 1-5.1.

3. Assume that the industry markup percentage on *total manufacturing cost* you calculated above is 67 percent. How much would:

   a. Manufacturing costs per car have to go down on each model, sedan and compact, for CCC to match the industry markup? *Hint*: Either use algebra and the cost-plus pricing formula or trial and error with your spreadsheet solution to question 2b.

   b. Prices have to go up for each model, sedan and compact, to match the industry markup?

4. Prepare a *thorough* analysis, based on information in Case 1-5 and your answers above, to determine where CCC should focus its efforts. For example, should CCC reduce its profit on each car by lowering prices as George Olson suggests? Should it reduce material costs? Should it increase the price of each car? As part of your analysis, prepare a percentage income statement for CCC based on 2002 estimated figures in Exhibits 1-5.2 and 1-5.3. Use Exhibit 1-5.1 as a model.

5. Compute CCC's estimated 2002 contribution margin ratio. In Case 1-4 you calculated the variable manufacturing costs that are presented for you in Exhibit 1-5.2. Assume that $2,000,000 of selling expenses and $1,000,000 of administrative expenses are variable. *Hint*: Compute total sales revenue and total variable costs at CCC's budgeted 2002 level of production and sales.

6. Compute CCC's 2002 estimated breakeven sales level.

7. Discuss how likely it is that CCC will not attain a level of sales necessary to break even, if costs remain at the planned levels. In other words, will it take a large or small shortfall in projected sales to cause planned income to fall to zero?

Group Assignment 1-5

SAUDI GOLF CART ORDER

Group number _____ **Signatures of group members participating:**

_____

_____

Objectives

1. Introduce special order pricing concepts
2. Reinforce incremental cost concepts

A golf course developer in the Middle East, Saudi Sport, Inc., is proposing to purchase 1,000 compact units from CCC. Even though Saudi Sport is well aware of CCC's normal selling price of $17,000, it is offering to pay $8,500 per unit, half the normal selling price. Terms of this offer include (1) F.O.B. CCC's factory and (2) cash payments before shipment. F.O.B. stands for "free on board," which denotes where title and all risks and costs of shipping pass to the buyer. Therefore, title passes to Saudi Sport when the golf carts leave CCC's factory, and Saudi Sport assumes the shipping costs and risks at that time. Because the order is F.O.B. CCC's factory and there are no commissions, there are no variable selling and administrative costs associated with the order.

George Olson, vice president of marketing, is flabbergasted at the low offer price. "Why, the $8,500 selling price is below our production costs!" He suggests that the prospective customer "go fly a kite." Jena Butler, vice president of finance, advances a counter point. "George, we have more than enough production capacity to meet this special order and the growth in domestic sales for the foreseeable future. Perhaps we need to take a hard look at this proposal."

Sally Swanson, vice president of production, stated: "George, I can see your resistance to this proposal if these units were to somehow compete with our present dealer network. But these units would be exported to the Middle East to function as golf carts rather than as highway vehicles."

"It just occurred to me that our U.S. Federal Highway Standards need not apply to off-road vehicles. We can delete some parts!" added Jena. This will reduce CCC's material cost per compact by $300.

George responded, "You're making a persuasive case. We have excess capacity, no increased competition to our existing products, reduced material cost, and no legal problems on differential pricing for exports."

Requirements

1. Prepare an analysis of the impact that the Saudi Sports, Inc. order will have on CCC's planned year 2002 net income of $8,090,000 (see Exhibit 1-5.3). Show all your calculations. *Hint*: Initial computations may be done on a per-unit basis.

2. What four nonfinancial conditions should CCC explore before it makes its final decision? Does the Saudi order meet all of the conditions? Explain.

3. Recommend whether CCC should accept this special order. Explain.

Case 1-6

JOB-ORDER COSTING AT CALIFORNIA CAR COMPANY

Case Objectives

1. Introduce the specifics of job-order costing
2. Introduce students to the cost of goods manufactured statement
3. Demonstrate the linkage of product costing to the financial statements

Decision (Financial Reporting): What production costs will CCC report for March 2002?

THE PROFIT DISASTER

It is now early April 2002 and President David Gomez wants a ballpark estimate of CCC's March 2002 costs and gross margins. He has an assistant go into the accounting system and collect the March information in Exhibit 1-6.1. "This income is an absolute disaster!" was the response of David Gomez when his assistant handed him the March income statement. "When the bankers and board of directors see this they will take drastic action. We promised them a profit for March, not a huge loss. This loss is so large we will never come close to meeting our planned income of $8 million for 2002. We may have to close down the factory!"

Exhibit 1-6.1

Estimated March 2002 Net Income		
Sales (300 sedans and 100 compacts)		$ 8,000,000
March direct materials	1,539,159	
March direct labor	1,726,585	
March actual overhead (estimated)	4,094,473	7,360,217
Gross margin		639,783
March selling and administrative costs		1,940,000
Income (loss) before tax		$ (1,300,217)

Jena Butler, after talking to David Gomez, asks you to verify CCC's March income before tax. To do this you need to cost all March jobs and prepare a cost of goods sold schedule.

THE JOB ORDER COST SYSTEM

CCC uses a *normal job-order cost system* to determine the cost of manufacturing a sedan or compact car. This means that cars are costed by assigning *actual* labor and *actual* material costs to each car. Factory overhead, however, is assigned based on a *predetermined overhead rate* of $83 per DLH used, as shown in Exhibit 1-6.2. The computed costs of the cars are used to determine the cost of the ending WIP and ending finished goods inventories so that CCC's accountants can prepare monthly income statements and balance sheets. CCC also uses these costs to help set prices and evaluate performance.

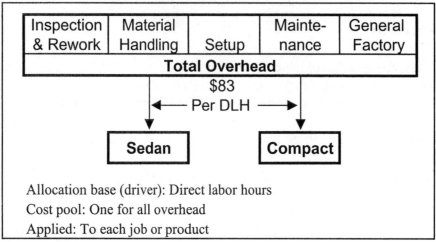

Exhibit 1-6.2
Traditional Overhead Costing at CCC

Allocation base (driver): Direct labor hours
Cost pool: One for all overhead
Applied: To each job or product

CCC chassis assemblers and final assemblers, who are classified as direct labor, carefully record the actual time spent working on each car model, sedan and compact, on forms called time tickets. Note that quite a few time tickets will be produced. If CCC has 200 direct labor employees and there are 20 work days during the month, then 4,000 time tickets will be created in that one month. A clerk must review each time ticket and copy the hours worked to the appropriate job cost sheet. The clerk then must look up the employee's wage rate and multiply the rate times the hours worked and enter that on the job cost sheet. This is a very tedious task.

Employees in material handling carefully record by model all direct material sent to assembly on material requisition forms. A clerk must copy these material costs to the appropriate job cost sheets. As a result, at the end of each month, CCC knows the actual direct labor and direct material costs for each model by simply adding up the labor and material costs that have been transferred to each job cost sheet.

CCC's controller has recommended that a networked microcomputer system be installed to replace the paper forms. In this system direct labor and material handling employees would simply enter the needed information into a computer. Total material and labor costs for each model would be determined each month by the computer without clerks completing all the forms and without transferring labor and material information to the job cost sheets.

To reduce the bookkeeping and computations required, CCC has simplified its cost accounting system so that it accounts for only four types of jobs per month:
1. The job that is in WIP at the beginning of the month,
2. All the sedan batches that are *both started and completed* during the month,
3. All the compact batches that are *both started and completed* during the month,
4. The job that is in WIP at the end of the month.

The four cost sheets for jobs that were worked on in March are presented as Exhibit 1-6.3a and b. Sedan Job 106 was in beginning WIP inventory on March 1, 2002. Sedan Job 107 and Compact Job 203 were started and completed during March; all work on these jobs was done in March. Sedan Job 108 was in ending WIP inventory on March 31. There were no compact jobs in March WIP beginning or ending inventories.

Exhibit 1-6.3a

CCC Summary Job Cost Sheet
Sedan Job 106

Batch size	15 Sedans		
Date started	2/26/2002	Date finished	3/3/2002
Date sold	3/14/2002		

Chassis Assembly Department

	Hours	Date	Cost
Direct materials		2/26/2002	$ 18,425
Direct labor	758	2/26 & 2/27/2002	26,530
Overhead applied		2/28/2002	
Total department costs			

Final Assembly Department

	Hours	Date	Cost
Direct materials		3/2 & 3/3/2002	$ 26,734
Direct labor	856	3/2 & 3/3/2002	29,960
Overhead applied		3/31/2002	
Total department costs			
Job totals		hours	
Average cost per sedan			

CCC Summary Job Cost Sheet
Compact Job 203

Batch size	125 Compacts		
Date started	3/2/2002	Date finished	3/30/2002
Date sold	(33 unsold on 3/31/2002)		

Chassis Assembly Department

	Hours	Date	Cost
Direct materials		Various March	$ 94,075
Direct labor	3,422	Various March	$ 119,770
Overhead applied		3/31/2002	
Total department costs			

Final Assembly Department

	Hours	Date	Cost
Direct materials		Various March	$ 326,475
Direct labor	4,729	Various March	$ 165,515
Overhead applied		3/31/2002	
Total department costs			
Job totals		hours	
Average cost per compact			

Exhibit 1-6.3b

CCC Summary Job Cost Sheet
Sedan Job 107

Batch size   360 Sedans
Date started   3/3/2002   Date finished   3/25/2002
Date sold   (86 unsold on 3/31/2002)

Chassis Assembly Department

	Hours	Date	Cost
Direct materials		Various March	$ 440,700
Direct labor	19,500	Various March	$ 682,500
Overhead applied		3/31/2002	
Total department costs			

Final Assembly Department

	Hours	Date	Cost
Direct materials		Various March	$ 632,800
Direct labor	20,034	Various March	$ 701,190
Overhead applied		3/31/2002	
Total department costs			
Job totals		hours	
Average cost per sedan			

CCC Summary Job Cost Sheet
Sedan Job 108

Batch size   15 Sedans
Date started   3/30/2002   Date finished   4/2/2002
Date sold

Chassis Assembly Department

	Hours	Date	Cost
Direct materials		3/30/2002	$ 18,375
Direct labor	790	3/30 & 3/31/2002	$ 27,650
Overhead applied		3/31/2002	
Total department costs			

Final Assembly Department

	Date	Cost
Direct materials	4/1/2002	(Next Month)
Direct labor	4/1 & 4/2/2002	(Next Month)
Overhead applied	4/30/2002	(Next Month)
Total department costs		(Next Month)
Job totals		(Next Month)
Average cost per sedan		(Next Month)

SUMMARY OF YEAR 2002 INFORMATION

You gather the following information useful in March job costs:
- The predetermined overhead rate for 2002 is $83 per DLH.
- All direct labor was paid $35 per hour in March.

Sales Information

CCC sold all cars completed except those in finished goods inventory. There were no sales returns or defective cars that were not repaired and shipped.

Finished Goods Inventory

CCC uses a first-in, first-out (FIFO) inventory flow assumption. This means that the car in inventory the longest is the first one sold. It also means that inventory is made up of the most recently completed units. Information on CCC's finished goods inventories is presented in Exhibit 1-6.4. Note that you must compute the March 31, 2002 ending finished goods inventory cost in order to complete the cost of goods sold statement.

Exhibit 1-6.4
Ending Finished Goods Inventory

	February 28, 2002	March 31, 2002
Sedans:		
Units	14	86
Cost	$221,200	You compute
Compacts:		
Units	9	33
Cost	$99,060	You compute

Requirements

1. Assume that sales revenue and selling and administrative cost numbers in Exhibit 1-6.1 are correct. What, if anything, is wrong with the March 2002 income calculation made for David Gomez showing a loss of about $1,300,000? You may want to come back to this question after you complete the other requirements.

2. Compute the costs for Jobs 106, 107, 108, and 203 as of March 31, 2002, by completing the outlined cells on the job cost sheets in Exhibit 1-6.3a and b.

3. Compute the cost of the March ending WIP inventory.

4. Compute the cost of the March ending finished goods inventory.

5. Prepare a cost of goods manufactured and sold (CGMS) schedule in the format given in Exhibit 1-6.5. *Be sure to link as many cells as possible in the statement to the job cost sheets* because it will make requirements 6 and 7 easier. See the Excel instructions for linking cells. Turn in this completed spreadsheet.

(Requirements are continued on the next page)

Exhibit 1-6.5

California Car Company
Cost of Goods Manufactured and Sold Schedule
March 31, 2002

Beginning inventory, finished goods

Cost of goods manufactured:

    March direct material

    March direct labor

    March manufacturing overhead applied

Total March manufacturing costs

Add: Beginning inventory work-in-process

Less: Ending inventory work-in-process

Cost of goods manufactured

Total cost of goods available for sale

Less: Ending inventory finished goods

Cost of goods sold

6. What is the impact on CCC's CGMS and ending inventories in WIP and finished goods if CCC used 500 more Chassis Assembly DLHs (at $35 per hour) for Job 107 than are shown in Exhibit 1-6.3b? Show the impact by printing a new CGMS schedule. Is the change in CGMS merely $17,500 (500 DLHs × $35)?

7. Return your spreadsheet back to where it was in Requirement 2 by eliminating the 500 additional hours you added to Job 107 in Requirement 6. What is the impact on CCC's CGMS and ending inventories in WIP and FG if CCC used 500 more Chassis Assembly DLHs (at $35 per hour) for Job 108 than are shown in Exhibit 1-6.3b? Show the impact by printing a new CGMS schedule.

8. Explain why the CGMS in your answers to Requirements 6 and 7 differ.

Case 1-7

VARIANCE CONTROVERSY AT CALIFORNIA CAR COMPANY

Case Objectives

1. Introduce the concepts of performance (flexible) budgets and cost variances
2. Introduce the use of managerial accounting information in performance evaluation

Decision (Performance Evaluation): How have CCC and its departments performed in March?

THE CONTROVERSY

It is now the middle of April 2002. After reviewing the cost of goods manufactured numbers that you prepared in Case 1-6, Sally Swanson, vice president of production, and Jena Butler, vice president of finance, meet on April 14 to discuss cost control. Jena says: "After comparing the actual March manufacturing costs with the March planning budget for manufacturing costs (as shown in Exhibit 1-7.1), I am concerned that our manufacturing costs are much higher than planned. If CCC is to earn an acceptable profit this year, it is critical that we meet our 2002 cost estimates."

Sally responds: "I am surprised the cost of goods manufactured schedule indicates that our cost control in March is weak. The plant ran smoothly in March and I know of no reason why our costs should be too high. Both of my production department managers and a couple of my overhead department managers are fuming. They all feel accused of not controlling costs when they are convinced they have done a good job. We better get to the bottom of all this before I have an outright revolt on my hands." Sally and Jena have asked you to evaluate the cost control performance of the production area in March as quickly as possible.

The accountants have given you Exhibit 1-7.1, which contains CCC's planned March production level of 468 cars (351 sedans and 117 compacts) and planned cost of manufacturing 468 cars. Exhibit 1-7.1 also contains the actual March manufacturing costs, as reflected in the March cost of goods manufactured schedule you prepared in Case 1-6. You can trace the actual direct material and direct labor costs back to the job cost sheets for March. It also indicates that total March *actual* manufacturing overhead cost is $4,325,229, as opposed to the March *applied* overhead of $4,094,473 that you used in the cost of goods manufactured schedule for Case 1-6. CCC considers the Inspection, Setup, and the Material Handling Departments to be variable cost centers. Costs in the Maintenance and General Factory Departments are considered fixed.

Exhibit 1-7.1

	Per Unit (Planned) (Case 1-4)	Planning Budget	Actual (Case 1-6)	Variance
California Car Company				
March 2002 Planning Budget Versus Actual Costs				
Units Produced: (Same in each production dept.)				
Sedans		351	375	24 F
Compacts		117	125	8 F
Sedan direct labor hours	108	37,908	41,180	(3,272) U
Compact direct labor hours	65	7,605	8,151	(546) U
Production Departments				
Chassis Department:				
Direct material cost				
Sedans	$1,220	$ 428,220	$ 459,075	$ (30,855) U
Compacts	750	87,750	94,075	(6,325) U
Direct labor cost				
Sedans (52 hours)	1,820	638,820	710,150	(71,330) U
Compacts (28 hours)	980	114,660	119,770	(5,110) U
Total Chassis Department		$1,269,450	$1,383,070	$ (113,620) U
Final Assembly Department:				
Direct material cost				
Sedans	$1,760	$ 617,760	$ 659,534	$ (41,774) U
Compacts	2,610	305,370	326,475	(21,105) U
Direct labor cost				
Sedans (56 hours)	1,960	687,960	731,150	(43,190) U
Compacts (37 hours)	1,295	151,515	165,515	(14,000) U
Total Final Assembly		$1,762,605	$1,882,674	$ (120,069) U
Overhead Departments				
Inspection Dept. (@$16 per DLH):				
Sedans	$1,728	$ 606,528	(1)	
Compacts	1,040	121,680		
Totals		$ 728,208	$ 774,500	$ (46,292) U
Material Handling Dept. (@$9 per DLH):				
Sedans	$ 972	$ 341,172	(1)	
Compacts	585	68,445		
Totals		$ 409,617	$ 435,825	$ (26,208) U
Setup Department (@$11 per DLH):				
Sedans	$1,188	$ 416,988	(1)	
Compacts	715	83,655		
Totals		$ 500,643	$ 559,575	$ (58,932) U
Maintenance Dept. (fixed):		$ 510,667	$ 498,460	$ 12,207 F
General Factory Dept. (fixed):		2,079,425	2,056,869	22,556 F
Total overhead		$4,228,560	$4,325,229	$ (96,669) U
March total manufacturing costs		$7,260,615	$7,590,973	$ (330,358) U
(1) CCC does not record the amount of actual variable OH by model.				
Total actual direct materials cost (from above)				$1,539,159
Total actual direct labor cost (from above)				1,726,585

Note that the first column of Exhibit 1-7.1 is information from Case 1-4. The material cost per sedan and per compact for each department is given at the top of Exhibit 1-4.2. The direct labor cost per car in each department is calculated by multiplying the hours shown in Exhibit 1-4.2 by $35 per hour. The 2002 predetermined variable overhead rate used in Case 1-4 is $36 per DLH. In Exhibit 1-7.1 the sum of the costs per DLH for the Inspection, Material Handling, and Setup departments is the same $36. The fixed overhead in Exhibit 1-7.1, the Maintenance and General Factory departments, total $2,590,092 for March. When this monthly total is multiplied by 12 months, it equals (with rounding) the estimated 2002 fixed overhead of $31,081,100 used in Case 1-4.

In Case 1-6 you found that CCC produced the equivalent of 375 sedans during March. They started and completed all 360 sedans in Job 107, plus they did all final assembly work on the 15 sedans in Job 106 and completed all chassis assembly work on 15 sedans in Job 108. The combination of work done on Job 106 and Job 108 is exactly equal to the amount of work required to produce 15 completed sedans. CCC produced 125 compacts in Job 203, all started and completed in March. These numbers are in the actual column of Exhibit 1-7.1.

Other numbers in the actual column also come from your solution to Case 1-6. The total March cost of direct material cost for both the Chassis Assembly and Final Assembly Departments totals $1,539,159 (summed for you at the bottom of Exhibit 1-7.1), the same number shown in the cost of goods sold schedule in Case 1-6. Likewise, the total March direct labor cost of $1,726,585 (49,331 DLHs) is the number you computed in Case 1-6.

The estimated (budgeted) 2002 information from Case 1-4 follows:

Material costs per car:	
Sedan	2,980
Compact	3,360
Direct labor costs per car:	
Sedan	3,780 (108 hours)
Compact	2,275 (65 hours)

Planned and actual direct labor rate per hour:	$ 35
Predetermined overhead rates:	
Variable	$ 36 per direct labor hour
Fixed	47 per direct labor hour
Total	$ 83

Requirements

In answering the questions, refer back to your solution to Case 1-4.

1. Discuss whether you believe that the manufacturing cost analysis in Exhibit 1-7.1 is appropriate. Why are some department managers complaining?

2. Many numbers in Exhibit 1-7.1 are carried forward from previous cases. Identify which numbers are from other cases and which cases they are from.

3. Set up a spreadsheet in the format of Exhibit 1-7.1. Include a performance budget column and compute new variances so you have a complete cost performance report. Print your new spreadsheet.

(Requirements continued on the next page)

4. Prepare an analysis discussing:

    a. The overall cost control performance of the entire plant.

    b. The cost control performance of each manufacturing department:

        - Chassis Assembly

        - Final Assembly

        - Inspection and Rework

        - Material Handling

        - Setup

        - Maintenance

        - General Factory

5. If CCC actually produced 378 sedans and 126 compacts in March instead of the 375 sedans and 125 compacts shown in Exhibit 1-7.1 and *all actual costs remain the same*, by how much would the variances for each of the following departments change? *Hint*: you can copy your completed solution to a new sheet in your Excel workbook and change the actual number of sedans and compacts produced.

        - Chassis Assembly

        - Final Assembly

        - Inspection and Rework

        - Maintenance

6. On several different occasions in March, the production of compacts was halted because of stockouts of small solar panels. In each case the chassis and final assembly lines had to be changed over to sedan production temporarily until parts arrived from the outside vendor, at which time the lines were changed back to the production of compacts. As a result, more setups were required in March than expected. In the following table, indicate the impact of the extra setups on the March variances by placing a U for an unfavorable impact, an F for a favorable impact, and an N for no impact.

Variance	Impact (U, F, or N)	Explanation
Direct material		
Direct labor		
Setup overhead		

Group Assignment 1-7

OVERDONE OVERHEAD?

Group number _____ Signatures of group members participating:

_____

_____

Objectives

1. Understand overapplied and underapplied overhead
2. Emphasize the differences between applied overhead, planning budget overhead, and performance budget overhead numbers
3. Demonstrate the impact of operating events on variances

After reviewing the March 2002 performance report you completed in Case 1-7, David Gomez, president of CCC, is confused about March overhead costs. He notes that the planning budget for fixed and variable overhead combined is $4,228,560 while the actual overhead is $4,325,229. This is an unfavorable difference of $96,669, which David views as quite significant. Even more confusing is the $2,543,002 in overhead you reported on CCC's March cost of goods manufactured schedule in Case 1-6. Jena Butler has prepared the schedule shown in Exhibit G1-7.1 to summarize the situation.

Exhibit G1-7.1

California Car Company Overhead Numbers for March 2002			
Planning budget:			
Variable	Case 1-7	$ 1,638,468	
Fixed	Case 1-7	2,590,092	$ 4,228,560
Performance budget:			
Variable	Case 1-7	$ 1,750,500	
Fixed	Case 1-7	2,590,092	$ 4,340,592
Actual overhead:			
Variable	Case 1-7	$ 1,769,900	
Fixed	Case 1-7	2,555,329	$ 4,325,229
Applied overhead (from COGS schedule):			
Variable*	Case 1-6	$ 1,775,916	
Fixed†	Case 1-6	2,318,557	$ 4,094,473

*49,331 actual direct labor hours × $36

†49,331 actual direct labor hours × $47

Sally Swanson studies the March performance report and the cost of goods manufactured schedule and she is a bit confused. She asks for your help in understanding the various March 2002 overhead numbers.

Recall that the planned production for March was 351 sedans and 117 compacts, while the actual production was 375 sedans and 125 compacts. Average planned monthly production for 2002 is 425 sedans (5,100 ÷ 12 months) and about 142 compacts.

Requirements

1. Module 1 explores four important management decisions: Planning (Case 1-4), pricing (Case 1-5), financial reporting (Case 1-6), and performance evaluation (Case 1-7). Show Sally the primary decision purpose(s) for each of the three March overhead measures (planning budget, applied, and actual) mentioned by David Gomez by placing an "X" in the appropriate boxes (you can check more than one box in each row or column).

	Decisions			
	Planning	**Pricing**	**Financial Reporting**	**Performance Evaluation**
Planning Budget OH				
Applied Overhead				
Actual Overhead				
Performance Budget OH				

2. Explain why the March planning budget overhead differs from the March applied overhead for:

    Variable overhead:

    Fixed overhead:

3. Explain why the March applied overhead differs from the March actual overhead for:

    Variable overhead:

    Fixed overhead:

4. By how much is CCC's March overhead overapplied or underapplied? Explain.

5. Sally is aware of a production problem that occurred during March that caused fewer cars to be produced than scheduled. Four times during March production of compacts was halted when inspection discovered defects in the solar panels. Each time a solar panel was found to be defective, the line was shut down, to see whether other defective solar panels were in the process of being installed or were on the pallet in the final assembly area ready to be installed. As a result, CCC used more labor hours than planned for March production. Fortunately, CCC received credit from its supplier for all defective panels discovered. Indicate how this event would have affected the March labor, material, and overhead manufacturing variances and the amount of overhead applied during March by completing the following table. U indicates an unfavorable impact, F indicates a favorable impact, and N indicates no impact. The question is not asking for any calculations.

Variance	Impact (U, F, or N)	Explanation
Direct material		
Direct labor		
Variable manufacturing OH		
Fixed manufacturing OH		

I (Increase) or D (Decrease) for applied OH only

Total applied OH		

Module 1

Peer Evaluation of Group Members	Class Section	Group No.

Evaluator's Name _____

Module 1

In the table below, please indicate your estimate, in percentage terms, of the contributions that individual group members made to each of the group assignments listed. Each column should add to 100 percent. For example, if there are five members in your group and all were present for Group Assignment 1-2, you would divide the 100 percent among the five members, including yourself. If you felt that all group members were prepared to discuss the assignment and contributed equally to the solution, you would give each person 20 percent. If only four members were present and you felt that one particular member contributed twice as much as the other three, you would give the heavy contributor 40 percent and the other three members 20 percent. Any group member who was absent should be listed and given a zero percent.

| Group Members (List) | Group Assignment Number | | |
	1-2	1-5	1-7
Myself			
Totals	100	100	100

Fill in this sheet after each group assignment is completed and turn in at the completion of Group Assignment 1-7.

MODULE TWO

COST MANAGEMENT

Systems

Case 2-1

ACTIVITY-BASED COSTING AT CALIFORNIA CAR COMPANY

Case Objectives

1. Introduce the concept of activity-based costing
2. Demonstrate the use of activity-based management
3. Contrast ABC with traditional costing

Decision (Operating, pricing): Which overhead costs are too high?

This problem builds on two cases completed in Module 1: Cases 1-4 and 1-7. You should review those cases and your solution notes before completing this case. Exhibit 2-1.1 presents CCC's 2002 planning budget overhead costs first shown in Case 1-7. Note that in Module 1, CCC classified Inspection, Material Handling, and Setup Department costs as variable. Predetermined overhead rates per DLH used in Module 1 are shown in Exhibit 2-1.1. Although these costs last year varied roughly in proportion to DLHs, this does not necessarily mean that the appropriate cost driver is DLHs, particularly since the ratio of sedans to compacts produced last year remained constant.

THE PROBLEM

It is now May 2002. Mary Jones, head of accounting for CCC, is concerned that the traditional costing method used in Module 1 does not adequately reflect the true costs of making each model. In addition, Jones wants to produce data that will help focus efforts to reduce manufacturing overhead so that CCC's profitability can be brought up to industry norms. Therefore, she is considering the possibility of converting to an ABC approach for assigning various overhead costs to the company's sedans and compacts.

Overhead Costs Details

The first step in implementing the ABC approach is to perform a detailed analysis of each overhead activity in the company. Although not all costs associated with an overhead cost pool will vary with a single cost driver, CCC decides to select the one driver for each cost pool that it believes best causes the cost to occur. The five manufacturing overhead cost pools used by CCC were described in Module 1. The following information for each cost pool is the result of extensive discussions among the production, sales, administrative, and accounting employees. It is based on their knowledge of how work is done at CCC. Note that cost pools assumed to vary directly with DLHs (variable overhead) in traditional costing used in Module 1 are found to have drivers other than DLHs.

Exhibit 2-1.1

California Car Company
Traditional Overhead Planning Budget for 2002

Units produced	
Sedans	5,100
Compacts	1,700
Direct labor hours*	661,300
Overhead departments	
Inspection and rework department†	$ 10,580,800
Material handling department†	5,951,700
Setup department†	7,274,300
Total Variable Manufacturing Overhead	$ 23,806,800
Maintenance department	$6,128,000
General factory department	24,953,100
Total Fixed Manufacturing Overhead‡	$ 31,081,100
Selling and administrative costs	
Compact redesign	$ 2,550,000
Other selling and administrative costs	22,950,000
Total S&A Overhead	$ 25,500,000

*Total budgeted DLHs computed as follows:

5,100 sedans × 108 DLH per sedan =	550,800	DLHs
1,700 compacts × 65 DLH per compact =	110,500	DLHs
Total Budgeted DLHs	661,300	DLHs

†In Module 1, Inspection Dept. costs were applied to jobs at the rate of $16 per DLH, Material Handling Dept. costs were applied at the rate of $9 per DLH, and Setup Dept. costs were applied at $11 per DLH, which resulted in the predetermined variable overhead rate of $36 you used in Module 1. Although these costs were classified as variable in Module 1, for this case you should determine whether DLHs are in fact the best driver.

‡The total fixed manufacturing overhead presented in Case 1-4 was $31,081,100. The amounts shown for the two departments are 12 times the monthly estimated overhead costs presented in Exhibit 1-7.1.

Inspection and Rework (I&R)

Defects are found in almost all cars completed at CCC. Many cars require a minimum amount of rework, but some require many hours to disassemble and repair. Due to poor design and the delicacies of assembling the solar panels, the compact car has many more quality problems than does the sedan. As a result it takes twice as many hours on average to inspect and correct each compact (50 hours) than each sedan (25 hours). Therefore, CCC estimates that the sedans will require 127,500 inspection and rework hours (25 × 5,100) and the compacts will require 85,000 inspection and rework hours (50 × 1,700).

Material Handling

CCC employees found that material handling costs vary with the total number of parts used. Each sedan requires 25 parts, 15 in Chassis Assembly and 10 in Final Assembly (see bill of materials in Exhibit 1-1.1). Each compact requires 20 parts, 10 in Chassis Assembly and 10 in Final Assembly. Use these numbers even if the models you assembled in the simulation used a different number of parts.

Setup

Due to the complexity of the design, management believes that the compact requires more setup hours than the sedan, but setup hours are not recorded by model. CCC's production schedule requires one setup for each batch of 15 sedans and one setup for each batch of 5 compacts. CCC plans to manufacture 5,100 sedans and 1,700 compacts.

Maintenance

This cost is most closely related to the age and usage of the machines. Both the sedan and compact use approximately the same number of machine hours (30 machine hours) per car on the same machines. Do not confuse machine hours with direct labor hours.

General Factory

This cost is fixed for a wide range of production volumes. It also does not have one activity that drives the cost. In ABC applications there is usually one cost pool like this that does not have a good driver, so the situation with the general factory costs is normal. Since this cost is not caused by any single activity in the short run, you should allocate this cost on a basis that you believe is most reasonable to CCC's situation.

Selling and Administrative

CCC budgeted $2,550,000 of its year 2002 administrative expenses exclusively for the redesign of the compact chassis and solar panels. Compact development costs at this level are expected to continue for several years. All development costs for the sedan are funded by grants from the government and electric utilities, so there are no separate development costs for the sedan. Management believes that the driver for the remaining $22,950,000 of selling and administrative costs is the number of cars produced.

Requirements

1. Complete the unshaded, outlined cells in Exhibit 2-1.2 using the traditional, plantwide overhead allocation used in Case 1-4. The I&R cost pool allocation has been completed for you. Use it as a model. Note that the total manufacturing cost for the sedan and compact models should be the same as computed in Case 1-4.

2. Complete the unshaded, outlined cells in columns marked as steps 1, 3, and 4 in the top part of Exhibit 2-1.3. Select cost drivers for each of the five manufacturing and two selling and administrative overhead cost pools. Determine estimated driver usage for the year 2002, and compute year 2002 estimated cost per driver.

3. Complete an ABC analysis by computing cost per car in Exhibit 2-1.3 using year 2002 budgeted full-year data for the compact and sedan. Also, complete the target selling prices for each model based on a 67 percent markup on total manufacturing costs. This should complete your worksheet. Print the spreadsheet and cell formulas if you completed the assignment on a spreadsheet.

4. Complete the following ABC proof by using your solution to requirement 3 in the cost per car column. Multiply the cost per car by the number of cars to compute the total allocation. The total cost pool for each overhead cost calculated in the proof should equal the cost pool shown in Exhibit 2-1.3.

Proof:		Cost per Car	Number of Cars	Total Allocation
Manufacturing overhead:				
Inspection and rework (I&R):	Sedan	$ 1,244.80	5,100	$ 6,348,480
	Compact	2,489.60	1,700	4,232,320
	Total Cost Pool			$ 10,580,800
Material handling:	Sedan		5,100	
	Compact		1,700	
	Total Cost Pool			
Setup:	Sedan		5,100	
	Compact		1,700	
	Total Cost Pool			
Maintenance:	Sedan		5,100	
	Compact		1,700	
	Total Cost Pool			
General factory:	Sedan		5,100	
	Compact		1,700	
	Total Cost Pool			

5. Explain the major reasons why the cost per sedan and compact computed in requirements 1 and 3 differ so much.

6. Discuss what, if any, pricing or product deletion actions you would recommend based on your ABC analysis.

7. Are any operating problems highlighted by your ABC analysis? Briefly discuss each overhead cost that you believe looks out of line at CCC.

Exhibit 2-1.2

California Car Company
Traditional Costing Worksheet

ABC Calculation Steps:	(1)	(2)	(3)	(4)	(5) Sedan	(6) Sedan	(5) Compact	(6) Compact
Title	Cost Driver	Cost Pool	Total Driver Usage	Driver Rate	Driver Usage Per Car	Cost Per Sedan	Driver Usage Per Car	Cost Per Compact
Direct material	- - -	$ 20,910,000	- - -	- - -	- - -	$ 2,980	- - -	$ 3,360
Direct labor	Direct labor hours	23,145,500	661,300	$ 35.00	108	3,780	65	2,275
Manufacturing overhead:								
Inspection and rework	Direct labor hours	10,580,800	661,300	16.00	108	1,728	65	1,040
Material handling		5,951,700						
Setups		7,274,300						
Maintenance		6,128,000						
General factory		24,953,100						
Total manufacturing cost	- - -	$ 98,943,400	- - -	- - -	- - -		- - -	
Desired markup (67%)	- - -	- - -	- - -	- - -	- - -		- - -	
Target selling price	- - -	- - -	- - -	- - -	- - -		- - -	

Exhibit 2-1.3

California Car Company
ABC Worksheet

ABC Calculation Steps	(1)	(2)	(3)	(4)	Sedan (5)	Sedan (6)	Compact (5)	Compact (6)
Title	Cost Driver	Cost Pool	Total Driver Usage	Driver Rate	Driver Usage Per Car	Cost Per Sedan	Driver Usage Per Car	Cost Per Compact
Direct material	- - -	$ 20,910,000	- - -	- - -	- - -	$ 2,980.00	- - -	$ 3,360.00
Direct labor	Direct labor hours	23,145,500	661,300	$ 35.00	108	3,780.00	65	2,275.00
Manufacturing overhead:								
Inspection and rework (I&R)	I&R hours	10,580,800	212,500	49.792	25	1,244.80	50	2,489.60
Material handling		5,951,700						
Setups		7,274,300						
Maintenance		6,128,000						
General factory		24,953,100						
Total manufacturing cost	- - -	$ 98,943,400	- - -	- - -	- - -		- - -	
Selling and administrative:								
Special development		$ 2,550,000						
Remaining $28 million		22,950,000						
Full cost per car	- - -	- - -	- - -	- - -	- - -		- - -	
Total mfg. cost (above)	- - -	$ 98,943,400	- - -	- - -	- - -		- - -	
Desired markup (67%)	- - -	- - -	- - -	- - -	- - -		- - -	
Target selling price	- - -	- - -	- - -	- - -	- - -		- - -	

Group Assignment 2-1

A COST BY ANY OTHER NAME

Group number _____   **Signatures of group members participating:**

_____

_____

Group Assignment Objectives

1. Contrast ABC with traditional costing.
2. Develop a better understanding of the impact of ABC on cost numbers.
3. Explore the use of cost numbers in a discontinue product decision.

George Olson, vice president—marketing at CCC, comes to your office with the new ABC data you prepared in Case 2-1. "I can't believe you accountants! You just finished your cost estimates for year 2002 last December (in Case 1-4) that produced the traditional costs in Exhibit G2-1.1. Now, just four months later, you give me new ABC manufacturing cost numbers (computed in Case 2-1) also shown in Exhibit G2-1.1. When I apply the industry average markup on full manufacturing cost of 67 percent to the ABC costs, I get the target prices shown. I do not understand how costs can change so much! I need some explanation!"

Exhibit G2-1.1

CCC 2002 Manufacturing Costs		
	Sedan	**Compact**
Traditional costs (Case 1-4)	$ 15,724	$ 11,030
Activity costs (Case 2-1)*	14,210	15,572
ABC target selling prices (67% markup)	23,731	26,005
* Your ABC numbers may differ based on the drivers you selected.		

Requirements

Help George Olson out by addressing the following issues:
1. Did the cost estimates change because CCC changed the way it manufactured a car? In other words, was the factory rearranged, more productive equipment purchased, or other changes made? Explain.

Yes ☐   No ☐

2. If total manufacturing costs for CCC stayed the same ($98,943,400 as computed in Case 1-4), explain to George how the manufacturing cost of the compact model increased by more than $3,000, but the manufacturing cost of the sedan model decreased only by about $1,000. Use your solutions to Case 2-1 as the basis for your answer. Your answer must go beyond just saying that the cost drivers changed.

3. After reviewing the ABC information, David Gomez, president of CCC, is considering dropping the compact model because its manufacturing plus selling and administrative costs total about $20,447 ($15,572 manufacturing costs plus $4,875 S&A—see your solution to Case 2-1). This is about $3,447 more than the compact's $17,000 selling price. David asks Jena Butler for her recommendation.

    As a result, Jena Butler asks you to estimate the year 2002 manufacturing cost per sedan and the total cost of each overhead department if the compact is eliminated. Please help Jena out by completing the following schedule. Note that Jena expects total General Factory costs will decrease to only $20,400,000 because many of these costs such as depreciation will not decrease if the compact is eliminated. Use the costs computed in your solution to Case 2-1.

Annual Costs if Compact Is Eliminated		
	New Cost per Sedan	New Total Cost
Direct materials	$2,980	$15,198,000
Direct labor	3,790	19,329,000
Inspection and rework cost		
Material handling cost		
Setup cost		
Maintenance cost		
General factory cost		20,400,000
Total manufacturing costs		
Note: CCC plans to produce 5,100 sedans in 2002		

4. Should CCC eliminate the compact? Justify your answer.

Case 2-2

IMPLEMENTING A QUALITY PROGRAM AT CCC

Case Objectives

1. Introduce the concepts of continuous improvement and quality
2. Demonstrate the accounting changes that occur when a quality program is implemented
3. Develop a broader understanding of management control systems

Decision (Operating): How can CCC improve quality and reduce the costs?

David Gomez calls a meeting of CCC's top managers. David states: "I have read quality books by Deming and Juran as well as *The Six Sigma Way*.[1] I am convinced that CCC can improve its quality and reduce its cost of poor quality if we implement a quality program. What do you think about beginning a quality journey?"

Jena Butler, vice president—finance, replies: "Based on the ABC analysis performed in Case 2-1, I have concluded that poor quality is a major reason that CCC's profitability is below the industry average. I also read quality books and I believe that a quality program can really help CCC." "Great," says President Gomez, "Why don't you and your staff develop a report outlining changes CCC would need to make if a quality program is initiated. Let's meet again in a couple of weeks once it is completed." As a result of this discussion, Jena asked you to prepare the part of that report that relates to the manufacturing process.

Requirements

1. Who are the customers of the order fulfillment (primarily manufacturing) process? How should manufacturing decide what constitutes quality so that they will know specifically what to measure?

2. Identify the areas outside of manufacturing from which representatives should be recruited to serve on the order fulfillment continuous improvement oversight committee. For example, marketing should have a representative.

3. Identify at least three actions that Jena Butler and the accounting department at CCC should take to support the quality program.

4. Develop at least four process output measures for the manufacturing process that you think might be reasonable. Be very specific in defining these measures, and be sure you link them to CCC's strategy and key success factors: (a) product reliability, (b) cost, (c) customer service, and (d) product innovation.

---

[1] P. S. Pande, R. P. Neuman, and R. R. Cavanagh, The Six Sigma Way (New York: McGraw-Hill, 2000).

5. Performance budgets have been a key element of CCC's management control system since the company was founded because the variances play a critical part in evaluating the performance of each department and its manager. In Case 1-7 you completed a performance budget for CCC that included variances for each of CCC's seven manufacturing departments (Chassis Assembly, Final Assembly, and five overhead departments). In reality, hundreds of variances are calculated for each activity in each department. These detailed variances are used to evaluate individual worker performance. Jena Butler was wondering if the quality program would change this. Should this change? Explain why or why not.

6. Control charts. You have collected data for two areas in the factory: the inspection of the incoming solar panels and the one-quarter inch drilling operation. Based on this data you have prepared control charts, shown in Exhibits 2-2.1 and 2-2.2, for each area. What conclusions can you draw from each control chart? What actions should management take based on each chart?

Exhibit 2-2.1

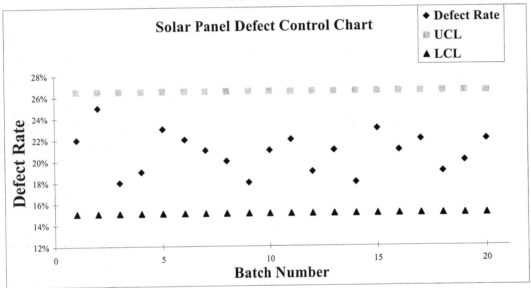

Exhibit 2-2.2

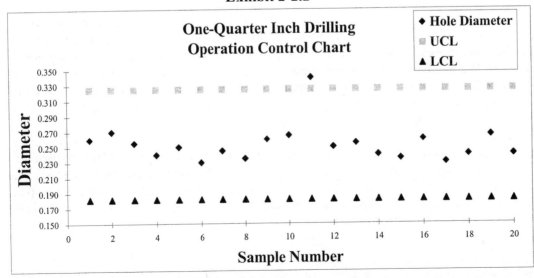

Case 2-3

COST OF QUALITY AT
CALIFORNIA CAR COMPANY

Case Objectives

1. Introduce students to the basics of COQ
2. Demonstrate the diagnostic and control uses of COQ information

Decisions: Where should CCC focus its quality efforts? Is the quality program successful?

Part I

It is now June 2002. David Gomez has reviewed the report on the impact of a quality program prepared under the supervision of Jena Butler. He calls an all day meeting of CCC's top managers to discuss the proposal. Sally Swanson, vice president—production, says, "Quality is very important at CCC, but with our rapid increase in production, the level of commitment and time required to implement the changes in Jena's report is beyond what we can do. Besides, we produce quality vehicles now and all of our workers already are committed to quality. We won't be able to show the magnitude of improvement some other companies have. Finally, this program is going to be very costly and CCC just can't afford it at this time. For the next two years, let's instead concentrate on expanding our capacity."

At the end of the meeting David concludes, "I believe that implementing a quality program at CCC is critical. However, everyone must be convinced that this is of the highest priority or it will never succeed. A quality program is a major undertaking and I am also concerned about our ability to select projects that will have the greatest payoff. Jena, can you provide more evidence about the possible benefits of a quality program, as well as some guidance as to where we should begin, if we decide to go forward?"

After the meeting Jena returns to her office with David. Jena says, "The only idea I have to address your request is to undertake a cost of quality (COQ) analysis. This will tie up my staff for several weeks and also will require the cooperation and time of many other managers. We will have to let the installation of the accounts payable slip by another month to do the COQ analysis. What do you think?" David responds, "I really want to get the quality program launched, and if COQ can persuade others, it's worth it. Go for it!"

Jena assembles a team of 11 people, consisting of a management accountant, an engineer, a purchasing agent, one person from each production department, a person from marketing, and one person from each of the five overhead departments. She also assigns three accountants from her staff as support people. A month later the team has developed estimated COQ information for 2002 assuming no quality improvements are made. This analysis is presented in Exhibit 2-3.1.

Exhibit 2-3.1

CCC Year 2002 Cost of Quality Worksheet
(Traditional Accounting Classification in Parentheses)

		Supplier Quality		Assembly Quality		Equip. Reliability	
		%	$	%	$	%	$
Prevention Costs							
Design reviews (S&A)*	$ 68,000						
Preventive maintenance (Manufacturing)	163,000						
Vendor production specification review (Mfg.)	114,000						
	$ 345,000						
Appraisal Costs							
Inspection and testing of assembled vehicles (Mfg.)	$ 926,000						
Inspection and testing of purchased parts (Mfg.)	157,000						
	$ 1,083,000						
Internal Failure Costs							
Rework (Mfg.)	$ 9,497,800						
Scrap (Mfg.)	208,000	20%	41,600	25%	52,000	55%	114,400
Downtime due to quality problems (Mfg., partially)	1,538,000						
Safety stock to cover quality problems (Mfg.)	412,000						
Machine repair costs due to poor maintenance (Mfg.)	2,418,000						
	$ 14,073,800						
External Failure Costs							
Warranty claims (S&A)	$ 5,859,000						
Customer quality-related complaints (S&A)	258,000						
Profits on sales lost due to poor quality (Not collected)	17,577,000						
	$ 23,694,000						
Total Cost of Quality	$ 39,195,800						

* This cost is not related to any of the three initiatives.

How the Cost of Quality Estimates Were Collected

The team had to collect data from departments throughout CCC. Some data came from recorded manufacturing costs, some from recorded selling and administrative costs, and a few costs were not recorded at all. A description of how information on each type of cost was collected is presented, following the underlined label for each category. The costs of each category are the costs shown in Exhibit 2-3.1.

Design review costs are estimates of engineering time spent to review and modify product design to reduce defects in the manufacturing process. Vendor production specification review costs are estimated by purchasing agents in the Material Handling Department with the help of engineers. Preventive maintenance is the cost of performing routine cleaning and adjustment of equipment, as well as replacement of parts that show significant wear and tear. Both inspection and testing of assembled vehicles and inspection and testing of purchased parts are performed by inspectors in the Inspection Department and comes straight from the accounting records.

Rework is done by mechanics in the Inspection Department, and scrap is part of direct material cost, both of which are recorded in the current accounting system. Workers estimate that about 38 percent of rework is due to defective material used in assembling the car with the remaining 62 percent due to assembly errors. About 55 percent of scrap is caused by improperly maintained machines, 20 percent by defective parts, and 25 percent due to assembly errors.

Cost of labor idled by downtime due to quality problems is estimated by the percentage of time that direct labor is idle. Production supervisors estimate that about 42 percent of production downtime due to quality problems is the result of defective parts, 20 percent is due to assembly errors, and 38 percent is due to machine maintenance. The cost of safety stock to cover quality problems is an estimate made by the Material Handling Department. The need for safety stock is caused 45 percent by defective parts and 55 percent by assembly errors. The Maintenance Department estimates the machine repair costs due to poor maintenance.

Warranty claims are recorded by the current accounting system, and the costs of responding to customer quality-related complaints are estimated by the Marketing Department. The Marketing Department estimates that about 48 percent of warranty claims and customer complaints are the result of defective parts used in manufacturing the cars. The other 52 percent are due to assembly errors. Profits on sales lost due to poor quality is the "softest" and largest number in the analysis. This number is a rough estimate arrived at by tripling the warranty costs. George Olson believes that this is a conservative number because a reputation for quality problems will cause a large percentage of customers not to purchase cars from CCC.

The top managers at CCC are shocked when they see the COQ information. Gomez comments: "Our quality costs are over 30 percent of sales. This is about five times our projected profit. We can double net income if we can reduce our quality costs by only 20 percent. Even if the profits from lost sales due to poor quality is excluded, quality costs are about 16 percent of sales and more than five times estimated 2002 net income! We need a plan for reducing the quality costs."

Requirements

1. Based on the COQ analysis Jena's staff performed, presented in column 1 of Exhibit 2-3.1, prepare a one-paragraph memo to David Gomez discussing whether David can justify a quality program based on potential cost savings.

2. You have been assigned the task of evaluating the potential cost savings from three quality initiatives that various CCC managers have identified as potential high priority projects: (a) improved supplier quality, (b) building quality into the product the first time, and (c) improved equipment reliability. Compute the quality costs related to each project. Use the cost numbers from Exhibit 2-3.1 and the description of each of these costs presented earlier. The cost of scrap that can be impacted by each of the initiatives has been entered into the solution template as an example of how to approach this requirement. *Hint*: Not every quality cost is related to one of the three initiatives. If no percentages are given for breakdown of a quality cost between categories, the entire cost should be assigned to one category.

3. Do you recommend that CCC spend more in any COQ areas? Identify the areas and explain why you would increase spending. How can costs in one category affect the level of costs in other categories?

4. David Gomez has reviewed your analysis and believes that one quality initiative that CCC should undertake is improving the quality of incoming parts from suppliers. The Purchasing Department estimates that it will cost $500,000 to set up a vendor review and certification (VR&C) program and $100,000 per year to administer it each year thereafter. It is estimated that the VR&C program will eliminate 80 percent of the defective parts CCC is now receiving. This in turn will allow the inspection and testing of incoming parts to be reduced by 80 percent. Although Gomez believes that improving vendor quality is important, he is concerned about the costs versus the benefits of the Purchasing Department's proposal. To save $117,750 (75% of $157,000) in annual material inspection costs, CCC must spend $500,000 this year and $130,000 each year thereafter. Should CCC pursue the VR&C program? Prepare an analysis showing why or why not.

Part II[1]

It is now February 2003. CCC has been working on the three quality projects described in Part I for almost one year. Sally Swanson and David Gomez questioned whether the efforts of management and employees to improve their products and processes were actually cost effective and resulted in improved reported net income. Jena Butler suggested that CCC estimate the *actual* cost of quality for 2002 and compare it to the estimated costs shown in Exhibit 2-3.1. In short, she suggested that CCC use cost of quality as a *process output measure* for the manufacturing process. As a result, the Accounting Department prepared this COQ information, which is presented in Exhibit 2-3.2.

Requirements (Continued from Part I)

5. Using the data in Exhibit 2-3.2, prepare a bar graph of the costs of quality, by category, both with and without a quality program. For example, your bar graph should show the prevention costs *without* the quality program next to the prevention costs *with* the quality

---

[1] This portion of the case was originally prepared by Matt Mouritsen.

program so it is easy to compare the two. Use the instructions in Case 1-4 for making an Excel chart (graph), but select *Column* instead of *XY Scatter*.

6. Analyze Exhibit 2-3.2 and the column graph made for requirement 5 and assess the impact of the quality program on CCC's costs during 2002. Is the quality program at CCC showing results? Based on the category information in Exhibit 2-3.2, discuss specific activities that you believe have contributed or not contributed to the improvement of quality at CCC.

Exhibit 2-3.2

2002 Cost of Quality for CCC With and Without Quality Program		
	Estimated Without Program	Actual With Program
Prevention costs		
Design reviews	$ 68,000	$ 347,000
Preventive maintenance	163,000	473,000
Vendor production specification review	114,000	644,000
	$ 345,000	$ 1,464,000
Appraisal costs		
Inspection and testing of assembled vehicles	$ 926,000	$ 691,000
Inspection and testing of purchased parts	157,000	101,000
	$ 1,083,000	$ 792,000
Internal failure costs		
Rework	$ 9,497,800	$ 5,287,000
Scrap	208,000	173,000
Downtime due to quality problems	1,538,000	887,000
Safety stock to cover quality problems	412,000	314,000
Machine repair costs due to poor maintenance	2,418,000	1,733,000
	$ 14,073,800	$ 8,394,000
External failure costs		
Warranty claims	$ 5,859,000	$ 3,744,000
Customer quality-related complaints	258,000	146,000
Profits on sales lost due to poor quality	17,577,000	11,232,000
	$ 23,694,000	$ 15,122,000
Total cost of quality	$ 39,195,800	$ 25,772,000

Case 2-4

IMPLEMENTING JUST-IN-TIME
AT CALIFORNIA CAR COMPANY

Case Objectives

1. Introduce students to basic production concepts in a JIT plant setting
2. Demonstrate the impact of JIT on accounting numbers
3. Introduce the basics of process costing

Decision (Operating): Does JIT improve manufacturing effectiveness?

INTRODUCTION

Toyota's Prius and Honda's Insight hybrid vehicles are priced less than similar CCC cars, while receiving high-quality ratings. As a result, CCC's management accepted the recommendation of Sally Swanson to adopt JIT ideas as soon as possible to compete successfully with Toyota.

In August 2002, during the two-week period in which most employees take vacation, CCC drastically modified its plant layout to the format shown in Exhibit 2-4.1. In addition, the company developed and introduced a Kanban system for scheduling production according to customer demand.

A Kanban is simply a card that authorizes a work cell to produce a unit or batch of units. A series of Kanban cards will be used in CCC as follows. Every time a sedan or compact is sold, a Kanban card will be passed from the customer to the final assembly person for the model sold. The card informs the worker to begin final assembly of another car. *The final assembly worker will not begin production until a Kanban is received*. At the time the final assembler begins work on the next car, the worker also passes the Kanban card to the chassis assembly person who then begins production of a chassis. See Exhibit 2-4.2 for Kanban instructions. Note that CCC's Kanban system is set up for the production of one car at a time rather than for a batch of two or more cars. Therefore, in the simulation there should never be more than one sedan and one compact in the finished goods area.

To illustrate how these JIT concepts are carried out at CCC, a second, in-class simulation will be carried out to illustrate ideas. During this simulation, your group will once again assemble sedans and compacts. This time, however, CCC's production facility will be arranged in the work cell format similar to that shown in Exhibit 2-4.1. A schematic of the simulation layout is presented in Exhibit 2-4.3.

Exhibit 2-4.1
California Car Company
JIT Plant Layout

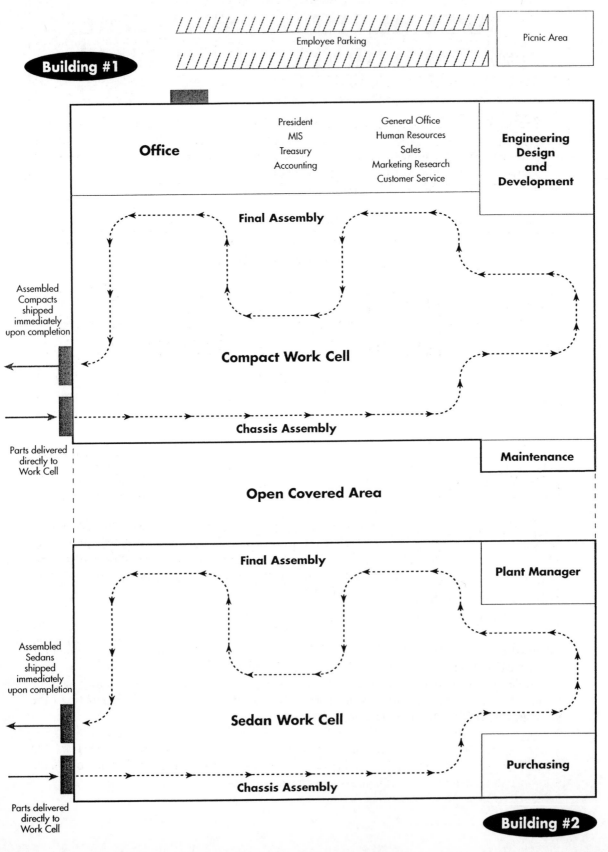

Exhibit 2-4.2
Kanban (Demand Pull) Instructions

1. The sales person, or customer if there is no salesperson, passes the Kanban card to the final assembler.

2. The final assembler takes the chassis from WIP and passes the Kanban card to the chassis assembler.

3. The chassis assembler takes the Kanban from the final assembler and gives it to the supplier when requesting more parts.

4. The supplier receives the Kanban from the chassis assembler, carefully files it, and delivers both final assembly and chassis parts for *one car only*. At the end of the simulation the Kanbans collected are given to the customer. The number of Kanbans given to the customer should equal the number of cars of that model sold plus defects.

Exhibit 2-4.3
Schematic of JIT Simulation Layout
(Arrows show the flow of parts and cars)

Note: Kanbans flow in the opposite direction of the arrows.

On the day of the CCC JIT simulation, each small group will assemble either sedans or compacts in a JIT work cell. For example, your small group may assemble compacts and the other small group you worked with on the first simulation will then assemble sedans. For assembly purposes, your small group is confined to a work cell and does not interact with the other work cell producing the other model.

If your instructor showed your class the Styro, Inc. video, you were able to see the positive impact a move to JIT can have. The statistics collected during the video are recreated in Exhibit 2-4.4. If you did not view the video, the statistics presented in Exhibit 2-4.4 will give you a sense of the impact JIT had on Styro, Inc.

Important Note

Some schools may be using sets of toy blocks that are different than those shown in this book. If so, your instructor will provide you with drawings for your set of blocks to replace Exhibit 1-2.2 and a new bill of materials to replace Exhibit 1-1.1.

STUDENT ROLES IN THE JUST-IN-TIME SIMULATION

Each student may be assigned one of up to ten different roles in the simulation. It is important that you study the responsibilities of your assigned role carefully so that your group can compete effectively against other groups. The simulation roles are listed on the next page.

1. Sedan parts supplier
2. Sedan chassis assembler
3. Sedan final assembler
4. Sedan salesperson
5. Accountant

6. Compact parts supplier
7. Compact chassis assembler
8. Compact final assembler
9. Compact salesperson
10. Customer

Exhibit 2-4.4

Summary of Styro, Inc. Video			
Numerical Results of Lot Size Reductions			
		Lot Sizes	
	8	**4**	**1**
Lead time or cycle time in minutes	5.1	2.4	0.5
Unfinished work-in-process inventory	43	19	4
Finished goods inventory	6	10	16
Quantity of potential rework	40	16	0
Space used (number of tables)	4	3	2
Average length of stockouts	2.4	1.2	0
Total units produced	36	26	22
Total production time (in minutes)	10	6	4
Average seconds per piece	16.7	13.8	10.9

Actions Taken to Reduce Lot Sizes
1. Rearrange the factory by reducing the number of tables.
2. Apply statistical quality control.
3. Reduce material handling by eliminating trucker.
4. Install universal die to eliminate setups.
5. Perform value-added analysis to eliminate waste.
6. Redistribute work among workers.
7. Implement preventive maintenance.

During the simulation, each student will act out one of the designated roles described below. The assembly of sedans and compacts will involve the same parts and the same assembly instructions as in the earlier simulation. See Case 1-1 for the bill of materials and assembly diagrams.

Suppliers

Each work cell in a production line has a supplier. Therefore, each line will have two suppliers, one for the sedan work cell and one for the compact work cell. The chassis assembly worker in each work cell will inform the supplier when the parts for a model have been used and more parts are needed by passing a Kanban to the supplier. The supplier will then deliver more parts to the appropriate workers in the work cell. For example, when the chassis assembler in the sedan work cell receives a Kanban card to initiate assembly of a chassis, he notifies the supplier by giving him the Kanban. The supplier promptly delivers parts for one chassis to the chassis assembler and parts to complete one sedan to the final assembler. The supplier should keep one set of parts for one chassis and one set of parts for final assembly in inventory to allow for prompt delivery to the work cell.

Each supplier must keep all Kanbans received during the simulation and give them to the customer at the end of the simulation. The number of Kanbans received by the customer must equal the number of cars sold from the work cell. If sales and Kanbans are not equal, it indicates that the line has not maintained JIT discipline, and is disqualified.

Chassis Assemblers

Each work cell in a production line has a chassis assembler. Therefore each company will have two chassis assemblers, one for the sedan work cell and one for the compact work cell. The chassis assembler will assemble the chassis for the work cell's model when a Kanban is received from the final assembler. *Assembly will not begin without the Kanban.* The chassis assembler will notify the supplier when work begins on a chassis by giving the supplier the Kanban so more parts will be delivered. This chassis assembler *carefully inspects* incoming parts and the assembled chassis.

Information You Must Collect for the Accountant

At the end of the simulation, estimate the percent of time you were idle while waiting for parts or a Kanban and record that percentage on Exhibit 2-4.5, item 8. The accountant will ask for this information at the end of the simulation.

Final Assemblers

Each work cell in a production line has a final assembler. Therefore, each company will have two final assemblers, one for the sedan work cell and one for the compact work cell. The final assembler will convert a chassis into a finished car for the work cell's model when a Kanban is received from the salesperson or customer. *Final assembly on a car will not begin without the Kanban card.* The final assembler *carefully inspects* incoming parts, the chassis, and the completed cars.

Information You Must Collect for the Accountant

At the end of the simulation, estimate the percent of time you were idle while waiting for parts or a Kanban and record that percentage on Exhibit 2-4.5, item 8. The accountant will ask for this information at the end of the simulation.

Accountant

During the simulation the accountant is responsible for collecting the cycle time measurement. Cycle time is computed by marking any sedan chassis, recording the time the chassis is marked, recording the time the marked chassis is moved from final assembly to finished goods inventory, and calculating the difference in recorded times. After the simulation has ended, the accountant is required to perform the following duties to complete Exhibit 2-4.5:

1. Record the number of sedan and compacts in work-in-process and finished goods inventories.

2. Collect from the customer the number of units sold by model, the number of stockouts by model, the number of defective cars by model, and the number of Kanbans received from the suppliers.

3. Collect from the chassis and final assemblers "idle time" estimates for the assemblers.

4. Calculate good units completed for both sedans and compacts. Good units completed = sales + cars in ending finished goods inventory – cars in beginning finished goods inventory.

5. Compute average production time per unit. To compute the average, determine the number of seconds the simulation ran, then divide that number by the total number of good units produced, sedan and compact combined. For example, if the simulation ran for 15 minutes and 25 good units were produced, divide 900 seconds (15 minutes × 60 seconds) by 25 cars, for an average production time of 36 seconds per car.

Finally, it is the accountant's responsibility to ensure that all members of the groups working on the production line have copied all of the information from the accountant's completed Exhibit 2-4.5 onto their own form. All students will need a completed Exhibit 2-4.5 to finish Part II of Case 2-4.

Salespersons

When informed of a sale, the salesperson physically gives the one sedan or one compact in finished goods inventory to the customer and initiates the Kanban system by passing a Kanban to the final assembler. This person should help collect sales and stockout data for the accountant. If your work cell has only four members, you will operate without this person. In this case the final assembly person will pass a car to the customer.

Customer

The customer draws a playing card (or some other sales marker) every 30 seconds. If you use playing cards, a club represents a compact sale, while spades, hearts and diamonds represent sedan sales. If there is a salesperson, the customer requests the proper model from that person. If not, the customer removes the model indicated from finished goods inventory and places the car in a separate sold-car area. At the same time he passes a Kanban to the final assembly person in that model's work cell. The customer next inspects the vehicle. If it is defect free, the playing card is then placed in the sold car stack. If the car is defective, place the card in a separate defect pile.

If a card is drawn and that model is not in finished goods inventory at the moment the card is drawn, then your line has a stockout. Place the card in a stockout pile that is separate from the sold car and defect piles. Once a stockout occurs the sale is lost forever. The customer *does not* convert a stockout to a sale as soon as that model is available again.

Drawing a playing card or sales marker begins as soon as the instructor tells your group to start the simulation. At the end of the simulation, the number of cards placed in the sold-car area plus the number of defects should equal the number of Kanbans received from the supplier. In addition, if the simulation runs for 15 minutes with sales occurring every 30 seconds, the total number of sold cars plus defective cars plus stockouts should equal 30. For your role *you will need a watch or clock that indicates seconds*. Customers should be selected from a competing production line so that customers have an incentive to enforce the JIT discipline and control quality.

Information You Must Collect for the Accountant

At the end of the simulation, you record the number of units sold *by model*, the total number of stockouts *by model*, and the number of Kanbans you receive from the suppliers on Exhibit 2-4.5. You give this information to the accountant when asked.

Part I Requirements (Complete Prior to the Simulation)

1. Review CCC's revised plant layout (Exhibit 2-4.1) and briefly identify major changes from the original plant layout in Exhibit I-2 (page 11). For each major change noted, briefly explain *why* you think CCC made the change.

2. Meet briefly inside or outside of class with your group to assign simulation roles to each member of your group. Briefly describe the role that you will be playing in the simulation.

Part II Requirements (Complete After the Simulation)

Prepare a one-page, single-spaced, typewritten analysis of the simulation that addresses the following:

1. A description of how the Kanban system actually worked for your job, within your work cell, and between your work cell and outside suppliers. Did sales equal the number of Kanbans collected by the supplier?

2. A brief identification of any weaknesses/inefficiencies in CCC's JIT operation.

3. A brief comparison of the JIT results with the results of the traditional manufacturing approach that you witnessed in carrying out the simulation in Case 1-2. Make comparisons using Exhibit 2-4.5.

4. An analysis of whether the JIT system has made CCC more competitive with Toyota. Identify specific improvements reflected in the JIT operation.

5. A brief identification of "process output measures" that you would recommend to CCC for use in evaluating work cell performance.

6. Complete Exhibit 2-4.5 and attach to your write-up. Data can be obtained from your group's accountant.

Exhibit 2-4.5

CCC Accounting Data Sheet
Comparison of Traditional and JIT Simulations

Student Group Numbers: Sedan [   ]   Compact [   ]

Results

	(1) Typical Traditional	(2) Your JIT	Percent Change*
1. Ending Inventory Levels:			
Work-in-Process:			
Sedan	8		
Compact	5		
Finished Goods:			
Sedan	8		
Compact	2		
2. Sales[1]			
Sedan	22		
Compact	7		
3. Stockouts[1]			
Sedan	3		
Compact	2		
4. Good Units Completed[1]			
Sedan	24		
Compact	7		
Total	31		
5. Defective Units[1]			
Sedan	4		
Compact	2		
6. Cycle Time (Sedan Only)	300 seconds		
7. Average Production Time			
Both models combined	38.7 seconds		
8. Assembler Idle Time Percentage			
Sedan	30%		
Compact	30%		
9. Kanbans Received from Supplier	N/A		N/A

*Difference between traditional and JIT results divided by traditional results:

(Column 1 – Column 2) / Column 1

[1] Based on running the simulation for 20 minutes

Group Assignment 2-4

JUST-IN-TIME SIMULATION
AT CALIFORNIA CAR COMPANY

Group number _____   **Signatures of group members participating:**

_____

_____

Group Assignment Objectives

1. Demonstrate the changes in production in a JIT setting
2. Link accounting information to changes in the production environment

Requirement

Group Assignment 2-4 is to perform the simulation for CCC using a JIT production layout. You will receive points for preparation and active participation. If anyone in your group did not prepare and/or did not actively participate, do not include his or her name above.

Have the accountant for your production line provide the information requested below, which was collected in Exhibit 2-4.5.

Total good units sold (both sedan and compact): _____

Total defective cars (both sedan and compact): _____

Total stockouts (both sedan and compact): _____

Total Kanbans held by the suppliers (both sedan and compact): _____

Case 2-5

JUST-IN-TIME COSTING AT CALIFORNIA CAR COMPANY

Case Objectives

1. Demonstrate the differences in product costing between JIT and traditional environments
2. Reinforce product costing and ABC concepts
3. Demonstrate with accounting data how JIT can improve manufacturing performance

Decision (Operating, financial reporting): Should CCC continue with its JIT initiative?

Assume that it is now early October 2002 and that CCC has fully implemented its JIT production approach. President David Gomez comes to Jena Butler and you very concerned.

> "I promised the Board of Directors and the bank that the September markup on total manufacturing costs would be at least 70 percent. My calculations show that we only had a 58 percent markup. This time I checked for changes in finished goods inventory, but units in finished good inventory remained unchanged during September. You reported that our quality program in conjunction with JIT has reduced our costs, but you were wrong! Our shareholders will not be happy."

David gives you the following calculations he prepared. Most of the numbers come from Exhibit 2-5.1.

September Markup Percentage Calculations			
	Sedan	Compact	CCC
Unit sales	360	120	480
Sales revenue	$ 7,560,000	$ 2,040,000	$ 9,600,000
Material costs	$ 1,067,040	$ 411,000	$ 1,478,040
Maintenance			124,000
General factory			400,000
Depreciation	425,000	170,000	595,000
Labor	2,800,000	591,500	3,391,500
Other overhead	51,000	21,250	72,250
Total manufacturing costs			$ 6,060,790
Markup percentage			58.40%

Jena asks you to get back to David ASAP either confirming or correcting his calculations. She also asks you to compute the cost of goods sold for CCC for the month of September 2002 in which 480 cars were produced: 360 sedans and 120 compacts. There were 60 sedans and 20 compacts in both the beginning and ending finished goods inventory. Cost of the beginning finished goods inventory was: sedans, $702,000; compacts, $200,000.

Exhibit 2-5.1

California Car Company
JIT Cost and Production Data
September and Estimated Full Year 2002

Production Information	Actual Sept. 2002	Revised Estimated Full Year 2002
Units		
Sedan	360	5,100
Compact	120	1,700
Direct materials cost (per car)		
Sedan	$ 2,964	$ 2,980
Compact	3,425	3,360
Work cell labor hours		
Sedan	80,000	969,000
Compact	16,900	204,000
Total work cell labor cost		
Sedan	$ 2,800,000	$ 33,915,000
Compact	591,500	7,140,000
	$ 3,391,500	$ 41,055,000
Work cell labor rate	$ 35	$ 35
Maintenance costs	$ 124,000	$ 1,463,700
Maintenance department hours:		
Devoted to sedan work cell	2,200	22,440
Devoted to compact work cell	900	12,410
Total maintenance hours	3,100	34,850
Depreciation costs		
Sedan work cell	$ 425,000	$ 5,100,000
Compact work cell	170,000	2,040,000
Total depreciation costs	$ 595,000	$ 7,140,000
Other work cell overhead		
Sedan work cell	$ 51,000	$ 612,000
Compact work cell	21,250	255,000
Total other overhead costs	$ 72,250	$ 867,000
General factory overhead	$ 400,000	$ 4,998,000

CCC still uses a FIFO inventory flow assumption. There was no *WIP inventory* in either work cell at the start or the end of the month. Both work cells had just enough parts in the *raw material* beginning and ending inventories to manufacture one car.

CCC now considers all work cell labor costs to be fixed (within the relevant range of expected 2002 production) and for managerial purposes treats labor costs like manufacturing overhead. Because CCC switched to JIT in the year 2002, the company has estimated how much overhead it would have incurred for all of 2002 if JIT had been implemented for the entire year. This estimate is based on the annual production of 6,800 cars for 2002—5,100 sedans and 1,700 compacts. The revised 2002 *estimated* data and the *actual* September 2002 data are presented in Exhibit 2-5.1. CCC is still asking $21,000 for the sedan and $17,000 for the compact.

Shared plantwide overhead consists of the Maintenance and General Factory departments. Since the implementation of JIT, CCC has installed a new maintenance information system that separately records and accumulates the number of maintenance hours spent repairing sedan work cell machines and compact work cell machines. General factory overhead includes all other manufacturing overhead not directly incurred by the work cells. CCC has elected to use total cars produced as the driver for the general factory overhead cost pool. Three types of overhead occur completely within the work cell itself: equipment depreciation, work cell labor, and other overhead, which includes indirect materials, and the work cell manager's salary.

Requirements

1. Is the analysis that David Gomez presented to you correct? Explain why or why not.

2. Select a cost driver for each of the shared manufacturing overhead costs in Exhibit 2-5.2 and compute the total shared overhead ABC cost assigned to each work cell.

3. Calculate the predetermined manufacturing overhead rate per car for the sedan and compact. Complete the September 2002 manufacturing cost per sedan and compact by completing Exhibit 2-5.2.

4. Compute CCC's September 2002 cost of goods sold (COGS) as well as the markup percentage based on COGS by completing the schedule in Exhibit 2-5.3. Be sure to link all of the September manufacturing costs and WIP inventory amounts in Exhibit 2-5.3 with the appropriate cells in Exhibit 2-5.2.

5. Why is the markup percentage you calculated different than David Gomez's? Write an explanation for David.

6. On average, CCC needs to produce and sell about 420 sedans and 140 compacts per month to meet its annual goal of 5,100 sedans and 1,700 compacts. Compute the markup percentage the way David Gomez calculated it, but use average monthly sales and production numbers of 420 sedans and 140 compacts. Why has it changed from David's original calculation?

7. If the September markup percentage in the cost of goods manufactured and sold schedule is actually on target, what issue related to your analysis should David Gomez be concerned with?

8. In Case 1-6 you costed sedans and compacts using a traditional job-order cost system. Describe two differences in how you costed the sedans and compacts in Case 2-5 compared to how you costed them in Case 1-6.

Exhibit 2-5.2

California Car Company
2002 JIT Costing Spreadsheet

	Cost Driver	Cost Pool	Estimated Total 2002 Driver Usage	Estimated Cost per Driver	*Total* 2002 Cost for Sedan Work Cell	*Total* 2002 Cost for Compact Work Cell	Total CCC Costs
Shared overhead:							
Maintenance							
General factory							
Direct work cell overhead:							
Work cell labor							
Work cell depreciation							
Other work cell overhead					—	—	—
Total 2002 estimated overhead cost							
Predetermined overhead rate per car							

	Sedan	Compact	Total
Scheduled 2002 production	5,100	1,700	6,800
September units produced	360	120	480
September materials used **per car**			
September overhead applied **per car**			
Sept. mfg. cost **per car**			

Exhibit 2-5.3

CCC Cost of Goods Manufactured and Sold Schedule September 2002		
Beginning finished goods inventory		
Add: Cost of goods manufactured:		
September direct material		
September manufacturing overhead applied		
Total September manufacturing costs		
Add: Beginning inventory work-in-process		
Less: Ending inventory work-in-process		
Cost of goods manufactured		
Total cost of goods available for sale		
Less: Ending inventory finished goods		
Cost of goods sold		
Markup percentage on total manufacturing costs		

Group Assignment 2-5

A COST IS A COST IS A COST?

Group number: _____ **Signatures of group members participating:**

_____

_____

Group Assignment Objectives

1. Reinforce an understanding of how and why costs changed at CCC
2. Reassess CCC's new competitive position based on its markup percentages

The top management team at CCC is delighted with the JIT costs for the sedan and compact you computed in Case 2-5. David Gomez states: "Our JIT and continuous improvement efforts have really paid off. Our costs are now at the level that will allow us to earn industry-average profits and attract capital needed to expand. However, I think we all need to fully understand why our costs per car changed so that we all have confidence in the numbers." Jena Butler's staff has prepared the following schedule to help you review these changes.

Exhibit G2-5.1

	Sedan			Compact		
	Traditional Est. Cost Case 1-4[1]	ABC Est. Cost Case 2-1[2]	JIT Cost Case 2-5	Traditional Est. Cost Case 1-4	ABC Est. Cost Case 2-1	JIT Cost Case 2-5
Cost						
Direct materials	$ 2,980	$ 2,980	$ 2,964	$ 3,360	$ 3,360	$ 3,425
Labor	3,780	3,780	6,650	2,275	2,275	4,200
Inspection	1,728	1,245	-	1,040	2,490	-
Material handling	972	921	-	585	737	-
Setup	1,188	713	-	715	2,140	-
Maintenance	1,001	901	185	602	901	307
General factory	4,075	3,670	735	2,453	3,669	735
Work cell depreciation	-	-	1,000	-	-	1,200
Other work cell overhead	-	-	120	-	-	150
Total manufacturing cost	$ 15,724	$ 14,210	$ 11,654	$ 11,030	$ 15,572	$ 10,017

Summary of Different CCC Cost Calculations

[1]The total traditional cost comes from the *planned* costs in Case 2-4, but the detailed breakdown of overhead costs was completed as part of Case 2-1 requirements.

[2]ABC costs are one of many reasonable solutions to Case 2-1. Also, ABC and traditional costs are estimates for all of 2002, while JIT costs are based on monthly production and costs.

Requirements

1. Compare the traditional and ABC columns in Exhibit G2-5.1 and explain why there are differences in manufacturing overhead costs per car. For example, are the differences due to changes in how the cars are manufactured?

2. Compare the ABC and JIT columns in Exhibit G2-5.1 and explain why there are differences in:
   a. The material cost per car.

   b. The labor cost per car.

   c. The overhead cost per car.

3. With selling prices of $21,000 for the sedan and $17,000 for the compact, calculate CCC's markup percentage based on total JIT manufacturing costs for the sedan and compact models. See Case 1-5 for a review of how to compute markup percentages.

4. Compute the overall markup percentage for *the entire CCC firm* based on JIT costs. CCC plans to produce 5,100 sedans and 1,700 compacts in 2002. Is CCC now earning the industry average of 67 percent markup on full manufacturing costs on each model and for the company in total?

5. Now that its profitability is above average, discuss three initiatives that CCC can undertake that would have been difficult for it to do previously. For example, CCC could begin paying dividends because its future profitability and cash flows are more assured.

Module 2

Peer Evaluation of Group Members	Class Section	Group No.

Evaluator's Name _____

Module 2

In the table below, please indicate your estimate, in percentage terms, of the contributions that individual group members made to each of the group assignments listed. Each column should add to 100 percent. For example, if there are five members in your group and all were present for Group Assignment 2-1, you would divide the 100 percent among the five members, including yourself. If you felt that all group members were prepared to discuss the assignment and contributed equally to the solution, you would give each person 20 percent. If only four members were present and you felt that one particular member contributed twice as much as the other three, you would give the heavy contributor 40 percent and the other three members 20 percent. <u>Any group member who was absent should be listed and given zero percent.</u>

Group Members (List)	Group Assignment Number		
	2-1	2-4	2-5
Myself			
Totals	100%	100%	100%

Fill in this sheet after each group assignment is completed and turn in at the completion of Group Assignment 2-5.

MODULE THREE

ANALYSIS OF FINANCIAL STATEMENTS IN A

Global Economy

Case 3-1

CALIFORNIA CAR COMPANY: PLANS FOR 2003

Case Objectives

1. Introduce the concepts of financial budgeting
2. Review the income statement
3. Develop spreadsheet skills

Decision (Planning): How should CCC prepare for next year? How much income do we plan to earn in 2003?

INTRODUCTION

In late October 2002, CCC's president, David Gomez, called a meeting of the company's Executive Committee: Dennis Madison, vice president–engineering, George Olson, vice president–marketing, Sally Swanson, vice president–production, and Jena Butler, vice president–finance. The purpose was to begin the development of plans for 2003. David began the meeting by asking Jena Butler to give the group a brief presentation on the expected financial results for the year ending December 31, 2002.

Jena began by passing out the financial information contained in Exhibit 3-1.1. She explained: "Net income for 2002 will be approximately $6.020 million, which is well below our budgeted amount of $8.090 million. Several factors account for this disappointing performance.

- Although sales prices of $21,000 for the sedan and $17,000 for the compact and a sales mix of 3 sedans sold for each compact sold have remained on target, sales volume fell short of our targeted amounts for both the sedan and compact. Competition from Toyota certainly appears to have hurt us here.

- Our production operations experienced numerous difficulties during the first half of the year, which resulted in significant cost overruns on units produced through July 31, 2002. Fortunately, our change to JIT in August led to improved efficiency, which prevented our income from being even lower.

- As our ending balance sheet is expected to show, the move to JIT will have a major impact on levels of ending inventories. Consequently, total assets will not be as high as budgeted. However, even with the significant reduction in inventories, we still fell short of our budgeted return on total assets (net income ÷ average assets)."

David turned next to George Olson and asked: "George, where do we stand with our competitors at the end of this year?"

George responded: "Jena correctly noted that we managed to maintain our sales mix at 25 percent compacts and 75 percent sedans, and kept selling prices constant at $17,000 for the compact and $21,000 for the sedan. Our problem is that our competition is beating us both on prices and on delivery times. In addition, we are still having problems with customer-reported defects that are hurting the sales of both models, but particularly the compact with its solar panel problems."

Exhibit 3-1.1

CCC Income Statements For Year Ended December 31, 2002		
	Budgeted[*]	Actual[†]
Sales revenue	$ 136,000,000	$120,000,000
Cost of goods sold	98,943,400	86,400,000
Gross margin	$ 37,056,600	$ 33,600,000
Operating expenses:		
Selling expenses	7,000,000	6,800,000
Administrative expenses	18,500,000	18,200,000
Income before taxes	$ 11,556,600	$ 8,600,000
Income tax	3,466,980	2,580,000
Net income	$ 8,089,620	$ 6,020,000

[*] From Exhibit 1-5.3
[†] Nine months actual plus Oct.–Dec. estimated

Sally Swanson responded, "George, we're going to be able to help you on all three counts next year. Our JIT approach is leading to significant reductions in production costs per unit, particularly for the sedan. This means that you will be able to be more competitive in pricing both models next year. Additionally, our cycle time has improved, and we are gradually solving some of our defect problems in both models. We are continuing to train our work cell personnel to become better inspectors at both the chassis and final assembly stages. Our vendor review and certification program should start showing results in 2003 also. Nevertheless, the solar panels on the compact may continue to be troublesome."

"I have been working closely with Solar Products, Inc., our supplier of solar panels," stated Dennis. "Based on our suggestions, they will alter the design of their panels next year in the hopes of reducing the number of defects that eventually show up in our completed compacts."

David Gomez concluded the meeting by observing, "Based on this discussion, I think we've got a pretty fair idea of where we will be at the end of 2002. We have also identified some good ideas to be considered in developing plans for 2003. Let's plan to reconvene in early December to complete our strategy for 2003. I want you to come to the December meeting with specific recommendations improving the following two items."

- Planned sales and production volumes in units and planned selling prices for both models for the year 2003. See Exhibit 3-1.2 for the results of a market research study recently completed for CCC by Accurate Market Research Company.

- Planned production costs per unit for each model.

Exhibit 3-1.2

Accurate Market Research Study Results Projected Market Shares for Year 2003		
LEV Industry Sales Forecasts:		
Sedans	90,000 vehicles	
Compacts	40,000 vehicles	
CCC Sedan Market Shares		
	Level of Advertising Expenditures	
Sales Prices	High ($70M)	Medium ($40M)	Low ($15M)
$ 21,000	11%	8%	5%
20,000	15%	11%	9%
19,000	21%	17%	13%
CCC Compact Market Shares		
	Level of Advertising Expenditures	
Sales Prices	High ($70M)	Medium ($40M)	Low ($15M)
$ 17,000	13%	10%	7%
16,000	15%	12%	10%
15,000	24%	18%	16%

DETAILED BUDGET INFORMATION

All managers at CCC identified the cost drivers for their department's costs and prepared an activity-based operating budget based on those drivers. The marketing department also developed CCC's sales drivers. The results of this operating budget effort follow. Some key drivers used in the budgeting process are:

Cost or Revenue	Driver
Work cell labor cost	Number of sedans or compacts
Maintenance cost	Maintenance hours
General factory cost	Number of shifts
Marketing cost	Level of advertising
Sales revenue	Selling price and advertising

Market Research

Accurate Market Research Company (AMRC) has determined that the 2003 demand for the entire LEV industry is 90,000 sedans and 40,000 compacts. AMRC then estimated the percent of total LEV industry demand CCC will achieve given various selling prices and advertising levels CCC can select.

To determine the number of sedans and compacts CCC can sell in 2003, first select CCC's advertising level, then select a selling price for the sedan and selling price for the compact. CCC can select only *one* advertising level for the entire firm. Therefore, if you select a medium advertising level for the sedan, you must also select a medium level for the compact. You can, however, select a $21,000 sedan price and a $15,000 compact price. The percentages in Exhibit 3-1.2 represent the share of each car market that CCC can expect to achieve. For example, if you select a low advertising level for CCC and a $20,000 selling price for the sedan, CCC would expect to capture a 9 percent share of the total sedan market, which is forecasted to be 90,000 vehicles. Thus, the estimated sales for sedans would be 8,100 cars.

Material and Labor Costs

The following information on work cell capacities, labor hours, labor rates, and material costs has been compiled for preparation of the 2003 budget. Material costs in 2003 are estimated to be the same as 2002 material costs: sedan, $2,980, and compact, $3,360. All labor is expected to cost $35 per hour. The sedan and compact labor requirements are summarized in Exhibits 3-1.3 and 3-1.4 respectively. Note that since CCC has adopted JIT, labor is now considered a step fixed cost rather than a variable cost.

Sedan Labor

As shown in Exhibit 3-1.3, the sedan work cell can produce up to 6,000 sedans per year with the current work cell labor force of 969,000 work cell labor hours (WCLHs) per year. The work cell output can be increased from 6,001 to 7,500 sedans per year by employing an additional 281,000 WCLHs per year. However, production levels of more than 6,000 sedans require implementation of a second shift in the sedan work cell. Note that the WCLHs required to produce 5,100 sedans is more than the 550,800 DLH computed in Case 1-4 because CCC has moved workers from support areas to the work cells after JIT was implemented. CCC's maximum two-shift sedan capacity is 12,000 sedans. You cannot produce or sell more than 12,000 sedans in 2003.

Exhibit 3-1.3
Sedan Work Cell Labor Hours

Annual Production Level	Number of Shifts Required	Annual Work Cell Hours Required
0 - 3,000	1	580,000
3,001 - 4,500	1	775,000
4,501 - 6,000	1	969,000
6,001 - 7,500	2	1,250,000
7,501 - 9,000	2	1,510,000
9,001 - 10,500	2	1,790,000
10,501 - 12,000	2	2,070,000
Note: 12,000 sedans are CCC's maximum two-shift capacity in 2003.		

Compact Labor

The compact work cell can produce 9,000 compacts per year with its current equipment and square footage of space. The compact labor requirements are summarized in Exhibit 3-1.4. CCC does not plan to operate a second compact shift.

Overhead Costs

Total overhead costs include manufacturing overhead as well as the period costs of selling, administrative, and income tax expense. Specific information regarding overhead costs follows.

Exhibit 3-1.4
Compact Work Cell Labor Hours

Annual Production Level	Number of Shifts Required	Annual Work Cell Hours Required
0 - 1,000	1	115,000
1,001 - 2,000	1	204,000
2,001 - 3,000	1	323,000
3,001 - 4,000	1	429,000
4,001 - 5,000	1	525,000
5,001 - 6,000	1	640,000
6,001 - 7,000	1	750,000
7,001 - 8,000	1	860,000
8,001 - 9,000	1	970,000
Note: 9,000 compacts are CCC's maximum capacity in 2003.		

Maintenance

Maintenance is expected to be $42 per maintenance hour, which is CCC's maintenance cost driver. CCC estimates that in 2003 they will use 4.4 maintenance hours per sedan and 7.3 maintenance hours per compact, which is a reduction from the hours per car used in 2002. The compact work cell requires more maintenance because it employs older, less reliable equipment.

General Factory Overhead

Plantwide overhead costs are expected to be $7,000,000 per year for a one-shift operation. Increased plantwide fixed overhead costs to add the second sedan shift are $3,000,000 per year due to the addition of a second shift plant manager and support staff.

Equipment, Depreciation, and Interest

To improve quality and reduce breakdowns, CCC plans to purchase and install, early in 2003, $108,000,000 of new equipment for the sedan work cell, which will be depreciated over 10 years with no salvage value. All existing equipment will be kept to improve the compact work cell and to reduce bottlenecks throughout the plant. Therefore, the current annual depreciation charges of $5,100,000 for sedan work cell equipment and $2,040,000 for the compact work cell will continue.

CCC and the equipment vendor have agreed that CCC will pay $108,000,000 plus $8,640,000 in interest expense on December 31, 2003. On December 31, 2003, CCC will obtain $64,000,000 from the bank in exchange for a note payable of that amount payable to the bank on December 31, 2006.

Marketing, Administrative, and Income Tax Expenses

Advertising expenses are based on your selection of a high, medium, or low level in Exhibit 3-1.2. Non-advertising selling expenses are expected to be $6,000,000 per year. In other words, the total marketing costs for 2003 are the sum of the $6,000,000 in non-advertising selling costs plus the level of advertising expenditures you select.

Due to continued major research and development efforts and general expansion, administrative expenses are expected to increase to $46,000,000 in 2003. CCC must pay a corporate income tax of 30 percent of reported net income before taxes in 2003.

Requirements

1. On a computer spreadsheet, prepare a budgeted income statement in the format shown in Exhibit 3-1.5. Save your spreadsheet electronically, because you will use it to answer Case 3-2. Make two copies of your printout so you will have one on which to write any corrections. The following detailed instructions should help you complete the budgeted income statement:

    a. Go to Exhibit 3-1.2 and first select an advertising level and then select selling prices for the sedan and compact. Enter these in the data table in Exhibit 3-1.5. The choice is yours, but try to select combinations that yield a high net income.

    b. Based on your selections, enter the market share percentages from Exhibit 3-1.2 in the data table.

    c. The industry sales forecasts are entered into the data table. Your instructor may have you change these numbers, however. Enter formulas in cells G8 and G9 to multiply the industry sales forecast by the market share percentage. This will produce CCC's demand for sedans and compacts, although it is possible that CCC may not be able to produce sufficient cars to meet that demand.

    d. If projected sedan sales in cell G8 are greater than 6,000, enter a 1 in the "shift =" cell (D9). If sedan sales are less than 6,000 units, enter a 0. You can make this happen with this IF statement: =IF(G8>6000,1,0)

    e. Enter Excel IF statements in the unit sales cells (C17 and C18) for the sedan and the compact. For example, cell C17 is: =IF(G8>12000,12000,G8). The IF statement will prevent your projected sedan sales from exceeding CCC's plant capacity of 12,000 units. The second IF statement should limit compact sales to 9,000 units.

    f. Go to Exhibit 3-1.3 and determine the number of work cell labor hours required to manufacture the projected sedan production in cell C17. Enter this number of hours in the "step labor hour: sedan" cell (D10). Do the same for projected compact sales, but use Exhibit 3-1.4 to find the work cell hours and enter them in cell D11. Note that work cell labor now is a (step) fixed cost. You can automatically enter the correct work cell hours for different projected sales levels in cells D10 and D11 if you build VLOOKUP tables in Excel, but it is not required. See the Excel help function for instructions.

    g. Complete the material, maintenance, and step work cell labor rows. All entries you make in columns C and D should have a cell reference to the data input table or to cells C17 and C18. If you don't enter cell references, Case 3-2 will be very time consuming.

(Requirements are continued after Exhibit 3-1.5)

Exhibit 3-1.5

	A	B	C	D	E	F	G
2			California Car Company				
3			Budgeted 2003 Income Statement				
4							
5	**Data Input Table:**						
6	Advertising level in dollars:				Market	Sedan =	%
7	Selling Prices:		Sedan =		Share %:	Compact =	%
8			Compact =		Unit	Sedan =	
9	Shift = (1 if second shift needed)*				demand:	Compact =	
10	Step Labor Hours:		Sedan =		Industry Sales	Sedan =	90,000
11			Compact =		Forecast:	Compact =	40,000
12			Tax rate =				
14			**Units**	**Price or**	**Subtotal**	**Income**	
15				**Cost**	**(Extension)**	**Statement**	
16	Sales:		Cars				
17	Sedan*						
18	Compact*						
19	Total Sales						
20	Variable Costs:		Cars				
21	Material: Sedan			$ 2,980			
22	Compact			3,360			
23	Maintenance:		Maintenance hours				
24	Sedan			$ 42			
25	Compact			42			
26	**Contribution Margin**						
27	Step Costs:		Labor hours				
28	Work Cell Sedan			$ 35			
29	Labor: Compact			35			
30	General Factory Overhead:						
31	First Shift						
32	Second Shift						
33	Other Fixed Costs:						
34	Depreciation:						
35	Sedan, Existing Equipment						
36	Sedan, New Equipment						
37	Compact						
38	Marketing and Advertising						
39	Administrative						
40	Interest Expense						
41	**Total Fixed Costs**						
42	Income before Tax						
43	Less: Income Tax						
44	Budgeted Net Income						

* Enter an Excel IF statement in cells surrounded by dashed boxes.

h. For general factory overhead, in the second shift cell, you want to multiply the additional cost of the second shift by cell D9 in the data input table. By doing this, the cost of the second shift will appear in your budget if cell D9 =1. If D9 =0, then your budget will show no second-shift cost. Cell D9 is called a binary variable, which is useful in constructing many types of spreadsheets.

i. If your income before tax is negative, then your income tax should be positive, which will reduce the amount of the loss. In other words, cell F43 should have the formula =(–D12*F42) and cell F44 should have =F42+F43.

2. Compute CCC's breakeven level of sales based on budgeted 2003 figures.

3. Compute CCC's 2003 budgeted markup percentage based on total manufacturing costs.

Case 3-2

CALIFORNIA CAR COMPANY: PLANS FOR 2003 (CONTINUED)

Case Objectives

1. Further develop budgeting concepts
2. Demonstrate how the financial statements are interrelated
3. Reinforce an understanding of balance sheets and cash flow statements

Decision (Planning): Can CCC finance its aggressive growth strategy?

THE PRICING DISAGREEMENT

At a weekly executive meeting George Olson, vice president of marketing, states, "Let's reduce the sedan selling price to $19,000 and the compact price to $15,000 and bump our advertising budget up to $70,000,000. Our sales force can really kick *&# at these prices and with that advertising exposure." "You will be giving up $2,000 per car based on our current prices," responds Jena Butler, vice president of finance. If we sell 20,000 cars next year, that is a loss of $40,000,000 in sales revenue. Since no costs will be avoided, net income before tax will decrease by $40,000,000! In addition, we will be forced to issue so much stock that we could lose control of CCC to outside investors. Let's keep our prices where they are and set advertising at $40,000,000." President David Gomez interrupts the disagreement: "Before we make any decision to lower prices dramatically, let's fully explore the financial implications."

President Gomez asks you to gather information about the financial impact of reduced prices. You have collected the following additional budget information.

Assets

Because CCC plans to increase sales significantly in 2003, it needs to make major asset acquisitions. The specific budgeted needs are presented in this section.

Accounts Receivable

To encourage dealers to stock more cars, CCC is not going to require payment on shipped cars for either 90 days or until the cars are sold, whichever is shorter. Therefore, CCC expects accounts receivable at the end of 2003 to be 20 percent of total 2003 sales.

Inventory

Inventory is expected to total $840,000 at the end of 2003.

Long-Term Assets

No long-term assets will be purchased or sold during 2003 except for the $108 million purchase of equipment described in Case 3-1.

Liabilities and Shareholders' Equity

The buildup in CCC's assets will need to be financed. As a result, liabilities and shareholders' equity are budgeted to increase greatly in 2003, as described in this section.

Current Liabilities

Total current liabilities are not expected to change during 2003, except for an increase due to income taxes payable. Each month's estimated tax expense is paid to the government by the fifteenth day of the following month. Therefore, on December 31, 2003, CCC expects to owe the government its December estimated taxes, or 1/12 of its total 2003 income tax expense. CCC will have no taxes payable at the beginning of 2003.

Long-Term Liabilities

Long-term liabilities at the end of 2003 will be the $64 million owed on the bank note.

Shareholder's Equity

CCC plans to declare and pay a $2,600,000 dividend in 2003. CCC plans to issue stock in increments of $1,000,000 to cover any cash shortage during the year. For example, if cash flow from operations, investing activities, and financing activities other than issuance of stock plus the beginning balance is a negative $2,450,000, CCC would issue $3,000,000 in stock.

Requirements

1. Correct the budgeted income statement spreadsheet you prepared for Case 3-1 and resubmit it.

2. Extend the Case 3-1 spreadsheet by including a budgeted 2003 cash flow statement in the format shown in Exhibit 3-2.1. Also complete a comparative projected balance sheet for 2003 in the format given in Exhibit 3-2.2. Note that the 2003 budgeted balance sheet and cash flow statement draw information from your income statement. Be sure that you link all three statements. In other words, some formulas in the cash flow statement and balance sheet should refer back to cells in the income statement. Thus, if you change one number, for example depreciation expense, all three statements should automatically be updated. Refer to Case 3-1 because you will need some of its information. Detailed instructions are presented below.

    a. Since they are interrelated, you can start with either the statement of cash flows or the balance sheet, but you can't complete one independent of the other. These instructions assume that you start with the balance sheet.

    b. You can't complete the ending 2003 cash balance until you complete the statement of cash flows, so skip to the 2003 accounts receivable balance and complete the cells for it and inventory.

Exhibit 3-2.1
California Car Company
2003 Budgeted Statement of Cash Flows

	A	B	C	D	E	F
5	Cash Flow from Operating Activities					
6	Budgeted income - 2003					
7	Add (deduct) adjustments to cash basis:					
8	Depreciation					
9	Change in accounts receivable					
10	Change in inventory					
11	Change in current liabilities					
12	Net cash flow provided by operations					
13	Cash Flow from Investing Activities					
14	Purchase of equipment					
15	Cash Flow From Financing Activities					
16	Sale of stock					
17						
18						
19	Cash flow provided by financing activities					
20	Net increase in cash and equivalents					
21	Cash at beginning of the year					
22	Cash at the end of the year					

c. When completing the ending 2003 balance in Long-term assets—net, think about what events increase or decrease this account during the year.

d. The ending current liabilities balance is simply the beginning balance plus 1/12 the income tax payable from your income statement. Be careful with the sign because a negative amount in income tax expense cell on your income statement is a positive expense and will result in an increase in current liabilities. If you should happen to have a negative income before tax on your income statement, the ending 2003 current liability balance should be less than the beginning balance.

e. The ending 2003 balance in contributed capital cannot be determined until you complete the cash flow from financing activities in the statement of cash flows. Leave the contributed capital cell blank for now.

f. Complete all blank cells in the statement of cash flows except sale of stock. Note that you need to identify two of the three cash flow from financing activities. Enter all formulas for subtotals and calculation of cash at the end of the year. At this point you should have a large negative balance in cash at the end of the year. You now need to enter in the sale of stock cell an amount, in increments of $1,000,000, that brings the cash at the end of the year to a positive number, but less than $1,000,000.

(Requirements are continued on the next page)

Exhibit 3-2.2
California Car Company
Comparative Balance Sheets

	A	B	C	D	E	F
					Budgeted	**Projected**
27						
28					**2003**	**2002**
29	Assets					
30	Cash					$ 1,462,000
31	Accounts receivable					13,600,000
32	Inventory					840,000
33	Long-term assets—net of depreciation					90,000,000
34	Total Assets					$ 105,902,000
35						
36	Current liabilities					$ 8,853,000
37	Long-term liabilities					10,000,000
38	Total Liabilities					$ 18,853,000
39	Shareholders' Equity					
40	Contributed capital					80,000,000
41	Retained earnings					7,049,000
42	Total Liabilities and Shareholders' Equity					$ 105,902,000

3. Create new budgeted income, balance sheet, and cash flow statements based on George Olson's recommendation of a $70,000,000 level of advertising and a selling price of $19,000 for the sedan and $15,000 for the compact. Use the market share percentages for this combination found in Exhibit 3-1.2, which is 21 percent for the sedan and 24 percent for the compact. Print your new set of financial statements. If you have built your spreadsheet correctly, this should involve changing only the following items:

   a. CCC's market shares for sedans and compacts: 21 and 24 percent,

   b. The selling price for sedans and compacts: $19,000 and $15,000,

   c. The level of advertising: $70,000,000,

   d. The number of labor hours, and

   e. The amount of stock that must be issued on the budgeted cash flow statement.

4. Create new budgeted income, balance sheet, and cash flow statements based on Jena Butler's recommendation of a $40,000,000 level of advertising and a selling price of $21,000 for the sedan and $17,000 for the compact. Use the market share percentages for this combination found in Exhibit 3-1.2, which is 8 percent for the sedan and 10 percent for the compact. Print your new set of financial statements.

Group Assignment 3-2

THE BEST LAID PLANS

Group number _____   **Signatures of group members participating:**

_____

_____ ___

Objectives

1. Demonstrate the linkage of financial budgets to the operations of a firm
2. Reinforce financial statement articulation

Assume that your budgeted financial statements for 2003 produced the following numbers:

Budgeted net income (after tax):	$21,000,000 (The income tax rate is 30%)
Cash at end of year:	437,000
Total assets:	252,000,000
Total liabilities and owners' equity:	252,000,000

Assume that CCC's contribution margin ratio is 80 percent.

Each requirement is independent. Use the original numbers given for each question.

1. Compute the new amounts for each of the following if CCC decides that it will declare and pay an additional $1,000,000 dividend in 2003.

   Budgeted net income: _____

   Cash at end of year: _____

   Total assets: _____

   Total liabilities and OE: _____

2. Compute the new 2003 amounts for each of the following if CCC sells 10 more sedans at $20,000 per sedan. Use the original numbers as a starting point. Assume that accounts receivable and accounts payable do not change.

   Budgeted net income: _____

   Cash at end of year: _____

Total assets: _____

Total liabilities and OE: _____

3. Compute the new 2003 amounts for each of the following if CCC decides to depreciate the $108,000,000 over 8 years instead of 10 years. Assume that this reduction in useful life does not change CCC's tax expense. In other words, the change in pretax income equals the change in net income after tax. Use the original numbers as a starting point.

Budgeted net income: _____

Cash at end of year: _____

Total assets: _____

Total liabilities and OE: _____

4. At a meeting to review the budget, David Gomez states: "The shareholders and bankers demand that we earn at least a $20,000,000 net income in 2003 and issue a maximum of $50,000,000 in new stock. Let's work on a budget that meets these requirements"

    a. Should CCC reduce prices to $19,000 for the sedan and $15,000 for the compact, while increasing advertising to $70,000,000 as George Olsen suggests? Refer to your solution to requirement 3 in Case 3-2.

    b. Should CCC keep the current prices for the sedan and compact and spend $40,000,000 on advertising in 2003? How can CCC meet David's constraints? Refer to your solution to requirement 4 in Case 3-2.

5. Discuss the advantages and disadvantages related to CCC's issuance of common stock versus borrowing all the cash needed to meet the 2003 budget.

Case 3-3

ETHICAL DECISION AT
CALIFORNIA CAR COMPANY

Case Objectives:

1. Review the steps in ethical decision making
2. Illustrate that management accountants are placed in a special ethical position

Decision (Financial reporting): Should the management accountant overreport the number of cars produced?

ETHICAL PROBLEM

It is now July 1, 2003. Assume that you are CCC's manager of cost management, an accounting position within the factory. Your department is responsible primarily for supporting the production management team headed by Sally Swanson, the vice president–production, who is your boss. You and the production people have been working together particularly hard for the past year. First you were involved with establishing an activity-based costing system that was instrumental in focusing attention on CCC's critical problems: setup costs and quality. You then were involved in designing the TQM and JIT systems that brought CCC's costs under control, greatly improving CCC's competitive position. Finally, you are working 60-hour weeks to implement a new balanced scorecard budgeting and performance evaluation system based on both financial and nonfinancial measures.

You purchased an expensive new home one year ago. The purchase stretches your family's finances to the limit, but CCC's bonuses give you a cushion. Unfortunately, your spouse was laid off last month and has no immediate prospects of landing another job. You are already one payment behind on the mortgage and without the bonus you may lose your house.

Over the past couple of years you have become very good friends with Sally Swanson and the other production people. You also have shared in the recognition and praise that the production team has received for the enormous improvements that have been made. Not insignificantly, you also have participated in sizeable performance bonuses that CCC has given the production group.

The six-month performance review is very important at CCC. Overall the JIT and TQM initiatives are working great. Demand for both the sedan and the compact has been strong. Due to supplier problems with the compact's solar panel and May parts shortages for the sedan, the production group was working feverishly to meet their demanding six-month vehicle shipment targets on June 30. After working overtime for two weeks, everyone thought that the production targets would be met. However, CCC's automated paint room broke down on June 30. As a result, the June 30 production runs of both sedans and compacts were not completed on schedule, but will be finished on July 1.

Missing the six-month production targets is very detrimental to morale and means that the production group will not receive a bonus. Since it is your job to report production figures to Jena Butler, vice president–finance, Sally Swanson calls you into her office. Sally explains how close production has come to meeting its targets. She also points out that the paint room problem is not major and that today, July 1, it will again be operative. As a result, CCC will be able to complete twice the normal daily production on July 1. Sally asks that you report the June 30 production as completed even though the cars were not painted until July 1. She argues that CCC will be better off because employee morale will be much higher, resulting in increased production and higher quality in the second half of 2003. She also points out that the overreporting is just a temporary, self-correcting issue, because total production numbers will be accurate after the doubled July 1 production. Finally, Sally appeals to you as a friend and dedicated production team member to help the group.

Requirements

Prepare a word-processed, single-spaced paper of at least one page in length that answers the following questions.

1. Address the following considerations you face in making your decision on whether to overreport June production:

   a. Relevant, significant facts

   b. Stakeholders

   c. Ethical issues involved

   d. Alternatives

   e. Consequences

2. Assuming that you are not a Certified Management Accountant (CMA) or Certified Public Accountant (CPA), would you report the higher production numbers that Sally Swanson requests? Explain.

3. Would your decision change if Sally threatened to fire you if you did not report the higher numbers?

4. Assuming that you are a CMA, would you have any additional professional ethical responsibilities in this situation? Cite any CMA professional code sections (the specific bullets) that apply from the *Standards of Ethical Conduct for Management Accounting and Financial Management* reprinted in Exhibit 3-3.1.

5. Explain why management accountants are placed in a particularly sensitive ethical position compared to production, marketing, and many other employees.

Exhibit 3-3.1
Standards of Ethical Conduct for
Management Accounting and Financial Management

Practitioners of management accounting and financial management have an obligation to the public, their profession, organizations they serve, and themselves to maintain the highest standards of ethical conduct. In recognition of this obligation, the Institute of Management Accountants (IMA) has promulgated the following standards of ethical conduct for practitioners of management accounting and financial management. Adherence to these standards, both domestically and internationally, is integral to achieving the *Objectives of Management Accounting*. Practitioners of management accounting and financial management shall not commit acts contrary to these standards nor shall they condone the commission of such acts by others within their organizations.[1]

COMPETENCE Practitioners of management accounting and financial management have a responsibility to:

- Maintain an appropriate level of professional competence by ongoing development of their knowledge and skills.

- Perform their professional duties in accordance with relevant laws, regulations, and technical standards.

- Prepare complete and clear reports and recommendations after appropriate analyses of relevant and reliable information.

CONFIDENTIALITY Practitioners of management accounting and financial management have a responsibility to:

- Refrain from disclosing confidential information acquired in the course of their work except when authorized, unless legally obligated to do so.

- Inform subordinates as appropriate regarding the confidentiality of information acquired in the course of their work and monitor their activities to assure the maintenance of that confidentiality.

- Refrain from using or appearing to use confidential information acquired in the course of their work for unethical or illegal advantage either personally or through third parties.

INTEGRITY Practitioners of management accounting and financial management have a responsibility to:

- Avoid actual or apparent conflicts of interest and advise all appropriate parties of any potential conflict.

- Refrain from engaging in any activity that would prejudice their ability to carry out their duties ethically.

- Refuse any gift, favor, or hospitality that would influence or would appear to influence their actions.

- Refrain from either actively or passively subverting the attainment of the organization's legitimate and ethical objectives.

- Recognize and communicate professional limitations or other constraints that would preclude responsible judgment or successful performance of an activity.

- Communicate unfavorable as well as favorable information and professional judgments or opinions.

- Refrain from engaging in or supporting any activity that would discredit the profession.

OBJECTIVITY Practitioners of management accounting and financial management have a responsibility to:

- Communicate information fairly and objectively.

---

[1] Institute of Management Accountants, "Standards of Ethical Conduct for Practitioners of Management Accounting and Financial Management," *Statement 1C Revised*, April 30, 1997. Reprinted with permission from IMA.

- Disclose fully all relevant information that could reasonably be expected to influence an intended user's understanding of the reports, comments, and recommendations presented.

RESOLUTION OF ETHICAL CONFLICT In applying the standards of ethical conduct, practitioners of management accounting and financial management may encounter problems in identifying unethical behavior or in resolving an ethical conflict. When faced with significant ethical issues, practitioners of management accounting and financial management should follow the established policies of the organization bearing on the resolution of such conflict. If these policies do not resolve the ethical conflict, such practitioners of management accounting and financial management should consider the following course of action:

- Discuss such problems with the immediate superior except when it appears that the superior is involved, in which case the problem should be presented initially to the next higher managerial level. If satisfactory resolution cannot be achieved when the problem is initially presented, submit the issues to the next higher managerial level.

- If the immediate superior is the chief executive officer, or equivalent, the acceptable reviewing authority may be a group such as the audit committee, executive committee, board of directors, board of trustees, or owners. Contact with levels above the immediate superior should be initiated only with the superior's knowledge, assuming the superior is not involved. Except where legally prescribed, communication of such problems to authorities or individuals not employed or engaged by the organization is not considered appropriate.

- Clarify relevant issues by confidential discussion with an objective advisor (e.g., IMA Ethics Counseling Service) to obtain an understanding of possible courses of action.

- Consult your own attorney as to legal obligations and rights concerning the ethical conflict.

- If the ethical conflict still exists after exhausting all levels of internal review, there may be no other recourse on significant matters than to resign from the organization and to submit an informative memorandum to an appropriate representative of the organization. After resigning, depending on the nature of the ethical conflict, it may also be appropriate to notify other parties.

Case 3-4

CAPITAL BUDGETING AT
CALIFORNIA CAR COMPANY

Case Objectives

1. Introduce the basics of capital budgeting·
2. Review time value of money and present value concepts

Decision (Planning): Should CCC invest $108,000,000, $74,000,000, or nothing in new equipment?

David Gomez, president of CCC, has been reviewing the 2003 financial budget and is concerned about the $108,000,000 investment in new equipment that is part of the budget. He states to Jena Butler, vice president–finance: "The $108,000,000 investment in new equipment is quite a commitment for CCC. Our net long-term assets at the end of 2002 are expected to total only $134,000,000. The new equipment is almost equal to our current investment in all of our assets! Are we sure that the benefits of the new equipment justify the investment? If purchase of the equipment turns out to be a major mistake, it could jeopardize CCC's financial stability. Can you have someone on your staff prepare a more detailed analysis of the new equipment purchase?"

Jena Butler has asked you to prepare an analysis of the new equipment purchase. Jena suggests that your first step is to talk to Sally Swanson, vice president–production, about the purchase. You schedule a meeting with Sally and ask her what the new equipment will do for CCC and if there are any other alternatives. Sally states:

> The new equipment will be installed during our end-of-year shutdown and will begin producing sedans on January 15, 2003. The equipment will make CCC a formidable competitor in the hybrid vehicle industry. The equipment is specially designed to be flexible, to be reliable, and to produce high-quality cars. By flexible, I mean that it will be very easy to manufacture cars with features that are special-ordered by individual customers. For example, if a customer orders a green convertible sedan with air conditioning and a CD player, we can economically build that car so the customer doesn't have to wait until we can produce a large run of similar cars.
>
> With respect to alternatives, we could purchase less flexible, less reliable equipment similar to our current machinery for about $74,000,000. This equipment, however, will seriously impair our efforts to implement a JIT system that is on a par with Toyota's current system or the capabilities of the other U.S. auto manufacturers. Both equipment purchases will increase CCC's production capacity to 12,000 sedans and 9,000 compacts per year. Without any new equipment, our production capacity will remain capped at its current level of 6,000 sedans (working two shifts) and 3,000 compacts per year.

After receiving this useful information from Sally, you decide to touch base with Jena to get a better feel for the parameters you should use in your analysis. In response to your question, Jena states:

> Since the new $108,000,000 equipment has an estimated useful life of 10 years, I suggest that you use a 10-year time period in your analysis. In addition, assume that the equipment will have a $4,000,000 economic (salvage) value at the end of 10 years, even though we will have fully depreciated it for financial statement purposes. When considering the $74,000,000 equipment, assume no economic value at the end of 10 years.

> Also assume that if no new equipment is purchased, annual cash flows from operations will be $8,090,000. If we purchase the new equipment, we will manufacture and sell 12,000 sedans and 7,200 compacts at a selling price of $19,000 and $15,000, respectively. This was management's final decision after reviewing the planning budget in Case 3-2. Assume this level of sales revenue for all 10 years.

The easiest way to compute the net increase in operating cash flows from the new investment is to:

a. Start with the estimated net income for each year. For your analysis use the budgeted net income for 2003 shown in Exhibit 3-4.2 for each of the 10 years for the $108 million alternative. Compute the $74 million alternative income by reducing the depreciation and increasing poor quality costs by $4,000,000.

b. Make the same adjustments to net income you do in an indirect statement of cash flows. For this analysis assume that inventories, prepaid assets, and current liabilities are unaffected by the equipment purchase. This means you don't have to make any adjustments for capital budgeting purposes. Assume that all expenses are paid for in the year incurred.

c. Accounts receivable is the odd account. It will increase by $46,000,000 at the beginning of the first year (year zero in the analysis), but there will be no other changes in the balance for the rest of the 10 years. Assume that there are no uncollectable accounts. At the end of 10 years, however, we will have $46,000,000 more accounts receivable than if we don't expand, so the correct way to handle this is to show on your spreadsheet a cash *inflow* of $46,000,000 in year 10 for accounts receivable.

d. A good way to show the incremental impact of the new investment is to enter CCC's $8,090,000 net cash flow if no new machines are purchased as a negative cash flow for each alternative. By including this, you have shown the net effect of the new equipment on the operations of CCC.

Your first reaction is that this is too much to absorb. Jena, however, helps you set up the format in Exhibit 3-4.1 and enters some numbers for you.

Requirements

1. On a spreadsheet, lay out the 10-year cash flows for the two alternatives: (a) purchase the $108,000,000 new equipment, or (b) purchase the $74,000,000 new equipment. Use the format presented in Exhibit 3-4.1. Note that years 2 through 9 are shown in one column to save space, but you will need to create in your spreadsheet a separate column for each year. CCC's income tax rate is 30 percent. Recall that the equipment will be

purchased by giving the vendor a note payable in the amount of $108M. Interest on this note *should not* be included in the cash flow analysis because how the equipment is financed is a separate decision.

2. Compute the net present value and internal rate of return for each alternative in Requirement 1. CCC uses a 17 percent discount rate in calculating net present value.

Exhibit 3-4.1
California Car Company
Discounted Cash Flow Analysis Format

	A	B	C	D	E	G
5	Alternative: $108,000,000 Equipment					
6			Year 0	Year 1	Years 2-9	Year 10
7		Cash Flows:				
8	Equipment purchase		$ (108,000,000)			
9	Operating cash flow:					
10		Net income				
11						
12	Increase in accounts receivable					
13	No purchase cash flows			(8,090,000)	(8,090,000)	(8,090,000)
14	Residual value					
15	Tax on salvage value					
16	Total net cash flows:					
17						
18			NPV =		IRR =	
19						
20	Alternative: $74,000,000 Equipment					
21			Year 0	Year 1	Years 2-9	Year 10
22		Cash Flows:				
23	Equipment purchase		$ (74,000,000)			
24	Operating cash flow:					
25		Net income				
26						
27	Increase in accounts receivable					
28	No purchase cash flows			(8,090,000)	(8,090,000)	(8,090,000)
29	Residual value					
30	Tax on salvage value					
31	Total net cash flows:					
32						
33			NPV =		IRR =	

3. Because of the significance of the investment, David Gomez has discussed the two options with the board of directors. The board strongly supports the $74,000,000 alternative because of its higher NPV. Prepare a one-page, word-processed analysis reporting your equipment purchase recommendation to David Gomez. Be sure to conclude whether CCC should (1) buy the $108,000,000 equipment, (2) buy the $74,000,000 equipment, or (3) buy no equipment at all.

(Requirements continue on the next page)

4. George Olsen believes that, based on CCC's improved quality and reputation and resulting ability to offer less generous terms, the level of accounts receivable can be reduced by $10,000,000 per year in each of the first four years of the project. This will reduce the year 10 inflow from accounts receivable to just $6,000,000. This reduction in accounts receivable will not happen if the $74,000,000 alternative is selected. Compute a new NPV and IRR for both alternatives under George's new assumption. Why did the NPV and IRR change so much when the total amount of the cash inflow for inventory in years 1 through 10 remain the same as before?

Exhibit 3-4.2
Budgeted 2003 Income Statement

	A	B	C	D	E	F
			Units	Price or	Subtotal	Income
14						
15				Cost	(Extension)	Statement
16	Sales:		Cars			
17	Sedan		12,000	$ 19,000	228,000,000	
18	Compact		7,200	15,000	108,000,000	
19	Total sales					$ 336,000,000
20	Variable costs:		Cars			
21	Material:	Sedan	12,000	$ 2,980	35,760,000	
22		Compact	7,200	3,360	24,192,000	59,952,000
23	Maintenance:		Maint. hours			
24		Sedan	52,800	$ 42	2,217,600	
25		Compact	52,560	42	2,207,520	4,425,120
26	Contribution margin					$ 271,622,880
27	Step costs:		Labor hours			
28	Labor:	Sedan	2,070,000	$ 35.00	72,450,000	
29		Compact	860,000	35.00	30,100,000	102,550,000
30	General factory overhead:					
31	First shift				7,000,000	
32	Second shift				3,000,000	10,000,000
33	Other fixed costs:					
34	Depreciation:					
35	Sedan, existing equipment				5,100,000	
36	Sedan, new equipment				10,800,000	
37	Compact				2,040,000	17,940,000
38	Selling					46,000,000
39	Administrative					46,000,000
40	Interest expense					8,640,000
41	Total fixed costs					231,130,000
42	Income before tax					40,492,880
43	Less: income tax					(12,147,864)
44	Budgeted net income					$ 28,345,016

Case 3-5

THE BALANCED SCORECARD
AT CALIFORNIA CAR COMPANY

Case Objectives:

1. Reinforce the concept of performance (flexible) budgets
2. Extend financial control concepts to include nonfinancial measures
3. Demonstrate the subjective nature of performance evaluation
4. Demonstrate the importance and dynamics of standard setting

Decision (Performance evaluation): How well did the work cells perform in 2003?

PERFORMANCE BUDGET INFORMATION

It is now mid-October, 2003 and Jena Butler's staff has gathered performance information for each of the work cells for the first nine months of the year. A summary of the actual performance information for each work cell is presented in Exhibit 3-5.2. In order to keep everyone working with the same numbers, use the sales and production data in Exhibit 3-5.2 rather than the figures you used for your Case 3-1 budget. You should, however, use the same unit costs per car that you used for your budget (see Cases 3-1 and 3-2).

Sedan Work Cell

Three significant budget events impacted the sedan work cell during the first nine months of 2003.

- A critical machine broke down in May, and all assembly had to stop for four production days until a replacement part could be obtained. The machine is rather old and heavily used. The cause of the part failure was a buildup of dirt from the routine operation of the machine.

- A supplier sent a batch of parts that had so many defects that the entire delivery was rejected, causing the work cell to shut down for two days until additional parts could be delivered.

- About 40 of the customer-reported defects involved a wiring problem that caused the headlights and taillights to suddenly stop working. Engineers redesigned the wiring in February, and no customer reports of electrical problems have been filed on sedans manufactured after this redesign.

Compact Work Cell

Two significant budget events impacted the compact work cell during the first nine months:

- The supplier of solar panels continued to ship many defective parts. Production was maintained only by having the supplier deliver far more solar panels than needed so that enough acceptable panels were always available in inventory. Nevertheless, approximately 25 percent of customer-reported defects for the compact involve faulty solar panels. The rest are due to assembly problems.

- In April the compact work cell adopted a "minimum line shutdown" policy whereby the line stopped only for absolute emergencies. The line was no longer shut down while a defect was corrected. Instead, a group of employees inspected and repaired the defective compacts after the compacts were completed. This change greatly improved cycle time and helped the compact work cell meet and exceed its production schedule.

Nonfinancial Performance Measures

CCC's actual performance on nonfinancial measures in 2001 and 2002 is presented in Exhibit 3-5.1. Based on the TQM and JIT changes implemented during 2002, the historical results presented in Exhibit 3-5.1, and extensive negotiations with the work cell employees, CCC has established the nonfinancial standards for 2003, also shown in Exhibit 3-5.1.

Exhibit 3-5.1
California Car Company
Nonfinancial Measures of Performance

	2001 Standards		2002 Standards		Budgeted 2003 Standards	
	Sedan	Compact	Sedan	Compact	Sedan	Compact
Percent late deliveries	30%	38%	19%	32%	8%	16%
Supplier defective part rate	4%	13%	6%	12%	3%	7%
Customer defect rate	5%	16%	4%	12%	2%	6%
Cycle time	11 days	14 days	6 days	12 days	5 days	8 days
Training hours percentage	3%	3%	3%	3%	5%	5%

Production and Sales

CCC is scheduled to produce 11,700 sedans and 6,400 compacts in 2003. By the end of September CCC is scheduled to have produced 75 percent of 2003's production. Therefore, production of 8,775 sedans and 4,800 compacts is scheduled through September 30, 2003. Projected cars sold through September 30, 2003 are equal to the projected production.

Actual production of sedans and compacts through September 30, 2003, totaled 8,446 and 4,930 cars, respectively. Actual sales through September 30, 2003, were 8,446 sedans and 4,816 compacts, as shown in Exhibit 3-5.2. Demand for sedans totaled 9,100 units through September.

Exhibit 3-5.2

California Car Company
Balanced Scorecard
For Nine Months Ended September 30, 2003

	Budgeted Unit Amount	Planning Budget	Performance Budget	Actual	Variance	
Sedan Work Cell						
Units produced	- - -	8,775		8,446		
Units sold	- - -	8,775		8,446		
Material costs	$ 2,980			$ 25,216,842		
Number of parts	25			212,678		parts
Labor hours	- - -	1,552,500		1,551,462		hours
Labor costs	$35/hr.			$ 54,611,462		
Late deliveries	8%			649		cars
Supplier defects	3%			6,394		parts
Customer defects	2%			148		cars
Cycle time	5 days	5 days		5.3 days		days
Training hours	5%			76,480		hours
Compact Work Cell						
Units produced	- - -	4,800		4,930		
Units sold	- - -	4,800		4,816		
Material costs	$ 3,360			$ 17,245,972		
Number of parts	20			99,834		parts
Labor hours	- - -	562,500		541,934		hours
Labor costs	$35/hr.			$ 19,130,270		
Late deliveries	16%			746		cars
Supplier defects	7%			7,772		parts
Customer defects	6%			386		cars
Cycle time	8 days	8 days		6.7 days		days
Training hours	5%			9,672		hours

Work Cell Labor

From Case 3-1, an estimated 2,070,000 work cell labor hours are required to produce 11,700 sedans, and an estimated 750,000 work cell labor hours are required to produce 6,400 compacts. As shown in Exhibit 3-5.2, projected work cell labor hours through September 30, 2003, are 75 percent of these annual estimates. The planned and actual work cell labor rates for a 40 hour week are $35 per hour. CCC pays time and a half for overtime, which is included as part of total actual work cell labor cost.

Requirements

1. Complete the following table by computing the full year 2003 budgeted level for each nonfinancial measure. Use production and sales of 11,700 sedans and 4,800 compacts as a basis for your answer. For example, the total budgeted number of late sedan deliveries is 936 (8% × 11,700). Sedans require 25 parts per car, and compacts require 20 parts. Note the units used for each measure in the last column. Some are cars, but others are parts, days, and hours. Within a reasonable range, will cycle time change as production varies?

Measure	Standard Rate		Planning Budget Full Year Amount		Unit of Measure
	Sedan	Compact	Sedan	Compact	
Percent late deliveries	8%	16%	936		Cars
Percent of supplier Defective parts	3%	7%			Parts
Customer-reported defect percentage	2%	6%			Defective cars
Cycle time	5 days	8 days			Days
Training hours	5%	5%			Labor hours

2. Is CCC using a balanced scorecard approach to performance measurement? Explain. Indicate to which of the four balanced scorecard perspectives each measure in the table is most closely related.

   For the remaining requirements, each group will be assigned a model (sedan or compact) and a perspective (work cell labor or management).

3. Complete the portion of CCC's nine-month balanced scorecard for the model assigned to your group in the format of Exhibit 3-5.2. For example, if your group is assigned the compact model, you need only fill out the compact (lower) portion of the performance budget. Use the 2003 standards shown in Exhibit 3-5.1.

4. Compute the work cell labor rate variance and the work cell labor efficiency variance for your assigned model.

5. Prepare a one-page, word-processed performance report from your assigned perspective (work cell labor or management) for your model. For example, if you are assigned the sedan model from the work cell labor's perspective, you will write the report to reflect as favorably as possible on your group, within the constraints provided by the available information. The management perspective group will try to hold the work cell accountable for results to the extent that the information permits. The case provides plenty of information on which to write a full-page performance analysis. Discuss each performance measure and the significance that you placed on each in arriving at an overall performance evaluation.

Group Assignment 3-5

SETTING STANDARDS FOR 2004

Group number _____ **Signatures of group members participating:**

_____

_____

Your group's model (sedan or compact): _____

Your group's perspective (management or labor): _____

It is now early November 2003. CCC must set new standards for 2004 so that the 2004 planning budget can be constructed. Jena Butler explains that the new standards should be set by having the work cell employee representatives negotiate with CCC's production managers. The negotiations should use the following quantitative information: (1) Year 2003 nine-month variances computed in Case 3-5, (2) Toyota benchmarks, and (3) standards from last year (2003). Non-quantitative factors will also enter into the negotiations.

Jena Butler has collected the following 2002 benchmark information for Toyota hybrid cars:

1. Percent of on-time deliveries to customers: 98 percent

2. Defective part rate from suppliers: .5 percent, or ½ of 1 percent

3. Customer-reported defect rate: 1 percent

4. Cycle time: 3 days

5. Percent of labor time spent in training: 6 percent

6. Total work cell cost: Unavailable, but Toyota used 100 work cell hours of labor to assemble a sedan and 70 hours for a compact

Requirements

1. Complete column 3 in Exhibit G3-5.1 before meeting with the opposing group. Use your answer to Case 3-5, particularly your evaluation of performance in 2003, as one input in setting the new standards. At the start of negotiations, obtain the opposing group's starting position for each standard record these figures in column 4. After the negotiations, complete column 5, the standards you agreed upon with your opposing group. Note that the numbers you offer as your first bargaining position often impact the final negotiated amount.

Exhibit G3-5.1
Your Negotiation Record

(1) Standards	(2) 2003 Standards	(3) Your Group's Consensus 2004 Standards	(4) Opposing Group's 2004 Standards	(5) Negotiated 2004 Standards
Labor hours per car	Sedan: 177 hours Compact: 117 hours	_____ hours	_____ hours	_____ hours
Late deliveries	Sedan: 8% Compact: 16%	_____ %	_____ %	_____ %
Supplier defects	Sedan: 3% Compact: 7%	_____ %	_____ %	_____ %
Customer defects	Sedan: 2% Compact: 6%	_____ %	_____ %	_____ %
Cycle time	Sedan: 5 days Compact: 8 days	_____ days	_____ days	_____ days
Training time	Sedan: 5% Compact: 5%	_____ %	_____ %	_____ %
Wage rate	$35 per hour	$_____	$_____	$_____

2. Summarize your team's justification for the year 2004 standards you proposed in column
   3 of Exhibit G3-5.1 for the following standards:

   a. Labor hours per car

   b. Customer defect rate

   c. Cycle time

Case 3-6

OPENING A FOREIGN SUBSIDIARY AT CALIFORNIA CAR COMPANY

Case Objectives

1. Understand foreign currency concepts
2. Become familiar with issues involved in operating a foreign subsidiary
3. Demonstrate a simple balance sheet consolidation of a foreign subsidiary

Decision (Investment): Should CCC open a subsidiary in Mexico?

PRELIMINARY ANALYSES

CCC's president, David Gomez, is a member of the board of trustees of the state university located near the company's headquarters. At an October 1, 2002, meeting, the dean of the College of Business, Catherine Collinsworth, proposed to Gomez that the university's international business students do a market research study to determine the sales potential of low emission vehicles (LEV) in various foreign countries.

In response, David Gomez stated: "Your proposal is timely, Dean Collinsworth, for two reasons. First, our new manufacturing process utilizing a JIT work cell approach has significantly enlarged our unit capacity, so we are looking to increase our sales. The other reason is that the rising value of the U.S. dollar in currency markets has allowed foreign competition to lower their prices. This is hindering our strategy to appreciably improve domestic market share. We have been contemplating a global market strategy but, frankly, we have not done sufficient research to make a final decision."

Dean Collinsworth replied: "David, let me suggest that our students do the research for CCC. The university's Internet access as well as substantial library resources should enable the team to assess the export potential for CCC's products. I will put Jeremy Schiller, professor of International Marketing, in touch with you. He is always looking for good projects for his students."

David responded: "There's one hitch, timing. We will need their report in 30 days if we are going to launch an export initiative in this budget cycle. We will need to forecast foreign sales so that manpower and material needs can be formulated. We will also need to get together with our banking and legal folks to determine policies and procedures to operate in foreign countries."

"Understood, David. I will present this deadline to Professor Schiller. I am confident that his students will deliver an excellent report within that time frame," said Dean Collinsworth.

Excerpts From the Student Export Report

Thirty days later the students presented their report to CCC. Excerpts from the report are presented here.

Factors creating demand for LEVs in foreign countries:

* Tax credits exist for persons buying a LEV.

* Highway infrastructure is sufficiently well developed.

* There is growing preference for auto transport over rail or bus.

* Auto purchase is affordable for over 25 percent of households.

Screening criteria for CCC's products:

* Average trip length is less than LEV's range—150 miles.

* Cost is less than half of annual household income.

* The banking system is well developed to facilitate auto financing.

* A one percent market share is equal to 1,000 or more units.

* LEVs are less than one percent of autos in the country.

The top three countries meeting the criteria:

Based on the study performed, sales projections for the three countries with the predicted demand are as follows:

| | **Sedan Demand Forecast** | | |
	India	**Mexico**	**Brazil**
High	5,000	3,000	2,000
Most Likely	4,500	2,400	1,500
Low	3,400	1,600	1,200

Limitations of the Study

The scope of the study did not include the differential variable and fixed costs that may be encountered in the various countries. Therefore, a ranking based solely upon demand criteria may not be the same ranking of profit potential in the three countries. Import duties, export licenses, commissions, freight, insurance, and sales costs may vary significantly in these countries. We recommend that these costs be determined and a comparative profit projection be made.

Management Meeting of November 10, 2002

David Gomez began the management meeting of November 10, 2002, by stating: "Last week Professor Schiller provided us the market research report authored by a team of his international marketing students. I trust all have studied the report and its recommendation. Let's go around the table for comments. George, let's hear marketing's input on this."

George Olson, vice president of marketing, responded: "The conclusions of the report appear to be backed up by solid data. There appears to be an unmet demand for cars like ours in the various foreign markets. However, I note that household income levels are considerably higher in Mexico than in Brazil or India. The government is achieving much-improved fiscal and monetary policies with the result that the economy has never been stronger. I recommend that Mexico be our initial foreign market to pursue."

Jena Butler, vice president of finance, interjected: "Let me second that. My staff researched shipping and insurance costs. From this analysis, Mexico is a market where we can deliver our products at very competitive prices. I estimate that it is going to take $1,000,000 to establish a marketing subsidiary in Mexico. However, Mexico is encouraging foreign investment and is willing to arrange local financing of 70 percent of the initial investment required. That means our cash requirement is $300,000. There is one catch. Mexico, like so many countries, has serious limits on how much currency can leave the country. We may not be able to pull profits out of Mexico for several years."

Dennis Madison, vice president of engineering, stated: "Multinational companies repatriate (bring cash back to the parent company) the return on their foreign investments by forming a vendor alliance in the country where they sell products. Our Mexican subsidiary could pay for certain components and ship them back here for assembly into our LEVs. We need to locate ISO certified suppliers in Mexico."

Sally Swanson, vice president of manufacturing, interrupted, "I have studied the demand forecast for Mexico provided by the student team. The expected market share means a production requirement of 2,400 units per year. In 2003 we are planning to run at 80 per cent of absolute maximum capacity of 12,000 sedans, or 9,600 sedans. To add production requirements beyond that is really impossible for 2003. I agree that we need to open new markets. The projected Mexican sale of 2,400 sedans brings us right to capacity. My recommendation is that we adjust our planned production to 12,000 sedans and try to meet both domestic and Mexican demand."

David Gomez said: "It appears we have a plan. We will enter the Mexican market with our sedan LEV, provided the projected financial results meet our goal of a 20 percent return on equity. Jena, please crunch the numbers to see if we can meet that criterion in Mexico. I need that report at 8:00 a.m. tomorrow."

Note: A discussion of foreign currency issues that will help in solving this case can be found at the web site for this book: www.csuchico.edu/acms/sadams_03

Requirements

1. Prepare a spreadsheet showing an opening balance sheet for the proposed CCC–Mexico subsidiary based upon the following transactions. Use the format shown in Exhibit 3-6.1. Requirement 1 asks you to complete columns 2, 3, and 4. Make sure your balance sheets balance.

   a. CCC–U.S. transfers $300,000 to CCC–Mexico as of January 1, 2003. Assume Jorg Hachenberger, CCC–Mexico's manager, converts the dollars into pesos using an exchange rate of 9.5 pesos/dollar.

   b. Jorg signs the necessary papers on January 1, 2003 to obtain a loan from the Bank of Cortez in the amount of 6,650,000 pesos.

2. Consolidate the effects of the above transaction with the balance sheet of CCC–US utilizing Exhibit 3-6.1. This requirement asks you to complete columns 5, 6, and 7.

Exhibit 3-6.1
California Car Company
Consolidated Balance Sheets for CCC–U.S. and CCC–Mexico
January 1, 2003 (Planned)

| | U.S. Parent | | | Mexican Subsidiary | | CCC Consolidated | |
	(1) CCC–U.S. Before Investment	(2) Investment Impact On CCC–U.S.	(3) CCC–U.S. After Investment	(4) CCC–Mex. After Loan & Investment	(5) CCC–Mex. Translation To Dollars	(6) Eliminations	(7) CCC Combined Balance Sheets
	$	$	$	Peso	$	$	$
Assets							
Cash	$ 1,462,000						
Accounts Receivable	13,600,000						
Inventory	840,000						
Long-Term Assets–net	90,000,000						
Investment in CCC–Mexico	0						
Total Assets	$105,902,000						
Liabilities and Shareholders' Equity							
Current Liabilities	$ 8,853,000						
Bank Loan to CCC–Mexico	0						
Long-Term Liabilities	10,000,000						
Total Liabilities	$ 18,853,000						
Shareholders' Equity							
Contributed Capital/Parent Equity	80,000,000						
Retained Earnings	7,049,000						
Total Liabilities & Equity	$105,902,000						

3. Jena Butler asks you to prepare a projected income statement for 2003 to estimate income of the Mexican sales subsidiary. In preparing the projection, several assumptions were given and are listed below. Use the format of Exhibit 3-6.2 to prepare the income statements.

Exhibit 3-6.2

California Car Company–Mexico
Budgeted Income Statement
Year Ended December 31, 2003

	Units	Unit Price (In Pesos)	Income in Pesos	Exchange Rate	Income in $
Sales	1,800	200,000	360,000,000		
Cost of sales	1,800				
Contribution margin					
Operating expenses			45,000,000		
Interest					
Income before tax					
Tax on income					
Net income					

a. Sale of sedan units will be less than the 2,400 originally forecasted. The development of effective advertising will take longer than anticipated, as is also true of prospective customer trust in the new product. Consequently, 1,800 units are forecasted to be sold in 2003, and 600 units will be in inventory at December 31, 2003.

b. CCC management decided to set the 2003 sedan price at 200,000 pesos. They plan an aggressive promotional campaign to introduce the LEV in the new market.

c. CCC–U.S. will ship CCC–Mexico sedan units using a transfer price of $14,000 each during 2003. The exchange rate used to record the intra-entity sales will be the forecasted average pesos/dollar rate for 2003. CCC–U.S. will ship 200 units to Mexico each month starting in January, 2003.

d. Forecasted 2003 exchange rates:

Beginning of year	9.5 pesos per dollar
Average for the year	10.2 pesos per dollar
End of year	11.0 pesos per dollar

e. Operating expenses are expected to be 45,000,000 pesos. Tax on income is 35 percent.

f. Interest on the loan from the Bank of Cortez is 13 percent per year.

4. Prepare a second income statement with the same information as in Requirement 3, except that the projected average exchange rate for 2003 is 11.2 pesos per dollar.

(Requirements continue on the next page)

5. If everything else remains as planned, to what level must the peso per dollar exchange rate change for CCC–Mexico to break even (earn zero income) in 2003? *Hint*: The only CCC–Mexico transactions that are not in pesos are the purchases of sedans from CCC–U.S. What is your assessment of the currency risk faced by CCC–Mexico?

Module 3

Peer Evaluation of Group Members	Class Section	Group No.

Evaluator's Name _____

Module 3

In the table below, please indicate your estimate, in percentage terms, of the contributions that individual group members made to each of the group assignments listed. Each column should add to 100 percent. For example, if there are five members in your group and all were present for Group Assignment 3-2, you would divide up 100 percent among the five members, including yourself. If you felt that all group members were prepared to discuss the assignment and contributed equally to the solution, you would give each person 20 percent. If only four members were present and you felt that one particular member contributed twice as much as the other three, you would give the heavy contributor 40 percent and the other three members 20 percent. <u>Any group member who was absent should be listed and given a zero percent</u>.

Group Members (List)	Group Assignment Number	
	3-2	**3-5**
Myself		
Totals	**100**	**100**

Fill in this sheet after each group assignment is completed and turn in at the completion of Group Assignment 3-5.

GLOSSARY OF KEY TERMS

Activity. A unit of work within a process. Preparing a customer invoice, repairing equipment, or preparing a midterm examination are examples of activities.

Activity-based budgeting. Budgeting costs by activity, with the intent to use the different activity costs to determine the cost of producing a product or providing a service. Thus, the focus of activity-based budgeting is on budgeting costs for activities, not by departments or other business segments.

Activity-based costing. The allocation of overhead costs directly to cost objects (products, customers, etc.) based on the cost drivers that cause costs to occur in overhead activities (maintenance, selling costs, etc.).

Activity-based management. The use of activity-based cost information to identify operational problems and to improve process effectiveness.

Activity improvement measures. Measures that provide guidance to employees on how to improve tasks or activities in a process. A statistical quality control chart is an example.

Additional paid-in capital. The difference between the par value of stock and the amount actually received by the firm when the stock is issued. Also referred to as contributed capital in excess of par.

Applied overhead. The assigning of overhead costs to cost objects through the use of predetermined rates rather than allocating the actual overhead costs incurred. The two main reasons for applying overhead rather than assigning actual overhead costs are timeliness of information for making decisions and the preparation of monthly or quarterly financial statements. The process of applying overhead involves a two-step method of computing the predetermined overhead rate and multiplying that rate by the amount of cost driver causing the overhead cost.

Appraisal costs. Costs incurred to check that products, processes, and services are in conformance with specifications. These include all costs to inspect incoming parts and goods and services produced. Appraisal costs also include quality audit and testing costs.

Attainable standards. Performance objectives that are challenging but achievable. Attainable standards are more motivating than impossible-to-achieve or easy-to-achieve standards.

Balanced scorecard. A performance report with measures, both financial and nonfinancial, that are linked to an organization's critical success factors.

Benchmark standards. Standards that are set with the idea of moving a firm's performance toward matching the world's best organizations at performing that activity.

Benchmarking. Evaluating the effectiveness of a process by comparing that process to the best similar process in the world. For example, many firms benchmark their sales order processing against L.L. Bean's sales order process.

Bill of materials. A list of the parts used in the manufacture of a product or component. It normally includes the quantity of each type of part used.

Book value. For an entire firm, book value is the accounting value of the firm's assets less the value of its liabilities. In other words, it is equal to the amount of a company's shareholders' equity section of the balance sheet. For an asset, book value refers to the purchase price of the asset less accumulated depreciation recorded for the asset.

Breakeven point. The level of either unit sales or total dollar sales at which a firm or product earns exactly zero income. It is computed by dividing total fixed costs by either the unit contribution margin (for the unit breakeven point) or the contribution margin ratio (for the breakeven in total dollar sales). Breakeven point formulas are:

Breakeven point in unit sales: $\dfrac{\text{Total fixed costs}}{\text{Unit contribution margin}}$

Breakeven point in total dollar sales: $\dfrac{\text{Total fixed costs}}{\text{Contribution margin ratio}}$

Budgeted balance sheet. A component of the financial budget that shows what the balance sheet will look like if budget assumptions were to become reality.

Budgeted cash flow statement. A component of the financial budget that shows what the statement of cash flows will look like if budget assumptions were to become reality.

Budgeted income statement. A component of the financial budget that shows what the income statement will look like if budget assumptions were to become reality.

Budgeting. The formalized, detailed process of planning for the future. The budgeting process normally includes the preparation of operating, capital, and financial budgets.

Capital budget. List of spending on approved projects that benefit the firm for more than one year. Examples include expenditures for plant and equipment, new product development, new information systems, and other long-term investments.

Cash flows. The amount of cash generated by a firm or an investment project. This is in contrast to accrual-based income for a firm, which is affected by noncash items such as depreciation and sales on account.

Committed costs. A special type of fixed cost that is locked in by past decisions and cannot easily be changed by future decisions. Depreciation on existing equipment is an example of a committed cost.

Comprehensive budget. A budget that includes both financial and nonfinancial measures. This is in contrast to a financial, budget that looks only at the financial dimension of planning and control.

Continuous improvement. An organizational philosophy which holds that, for every process, procedures should be established to assist employees in managing and measuring ongoing improvement to their process.

Contribution income statement. An income statement constructed such that the major headings are: sales, variable expenses, contribution margin, fixed expenses, and net income.

Contribution margin. Unit contribution margin is unit sales revenue minus unit variable costs. Total contribution margin is total sales minus total variable costs. Total contribution margin is also equal to total fixed costs plus net income.

Contribution margin ratio. Contribution margin divided by sales. This is total contribution margin divided by total sales or unit contribution margin divided by unit selling price.

Control. The management function that seeks to ensure that the plans are being followed and appropriately modified as circumstances change.

Control chart. A plot of data measuring some aspect of a process with control limit lines drawn three standard deviations from the mean. Control charts are used to differentiate special cause events from common cause events and to help employees tell if they are improving the process.

Controllable (noncontrollable) cost. A cost which managers can cause to increase or decrease through their actions. Note that a cost that is noncontrollable to one manager may be controllable to a higher-level manager. A key concept of responsibility accounting is that managers should be evaluated only on costs over which they have control.

Core processes. Processes that are part of a firm's value chain. Examples include product development, order fulfillment, and customer service.

Corporate performance measures. Comprehensive measures of performance for an entire organization or large divisions of a firm. Examples include return on equity and market share. The object of the management control system is to link process output measures to corporate performance measures in a way that is meaningful to process managers and employees.

Cost base. The group of costs that a company selects to use as the basis of cost-plus pricing. An example of a cost base is variable manufacturing costs.

Cost driver. The primary factor causing the cost of an activity to increase or decrease. For example, total setup costs may be driven by the number of setups performed.

Cost management systems. Information systems used to support managers in their efforts to improve efficiency and to better meet the needs of the customer.

Cost object. Anything which requires a measurement of the cost of inputs into that item. Cost objects may include products, services, activities, departments, programs, and even customers. The choice of cost objects depends on the type of decision to be made.

Cost of capital. The rate of return required to attract investors to invest in a firm.

Cost of goods manufactured. The direct material, direct labor and manufacturing overhead costs of units completed during the period. In a job-order cost system, this is simply the summation of job cost sheets for all jobs completed during the period.

Cost of goods sold. The cost of all goods sold during the accounting period. It is computed by adjusting cost of goods manufactured for the change in finished goods inventory. Cost of goods sold is the first major expense item shown on the income statement. Sales less cost of goods sold equals gross margin.

Cost of goods sold budget. This schedule summarizes all of the planned factory cost information regarding the cost of planned units produced and sold.

Cost of quality. Term used to identify the total costs incurred by an organization to prevent poor quality plus costs incurred due to poor quality. Includes cost of inspection and lost customer goodwill due to poor quality products. Most firms discover that the cost of quality is about 25 percent of revenue and several times the level of income.

Cost-plus pricing. The use of cost information to set a selling price or set a target selling price. The selling price is usually computed by applying a standard markup to some cost base.

Cost pool. The aggregation of similar costs for the purpose of cost allocation. It is desirable that all costs in a cost pool have the same cost driver.

Critical (or key) success factors. The few key things an organization must do well to implement its strategy successfully. For example, quality is a critical success factor for CCC because its strategy is to pursue a high-quality segment of the LEV market.

Cross exchange rate. The exchange rate between two currencies that is developed based on each of these two currencies' exchange rates with a third currency. For example, in Reading 5-1 the exchange rate between the South African rand and the Japanese yen was computed by using the current exchange rate between each currency to the U.S. dollar.

Currency devaluation. An action by a country to reduce the value of its currency relative to other currencies. This is done by increasing the amount (exchange rate) of domestic currency required to purchase foreign currencies.

Current exchange rate. The exchange rate at the balance sheet date.

Current ratio. Total current assets divided by total current liabilities. This ratio is a measure of a company's ability to meet its short-term debt obligations.

Cycle (or throughput) time. The time it takes for one unit to progress from the start of production to either completion of production or sale.

Debt-to-equity ratio. Total liabilities divided by stockholders' equity. This ratio is a measure of the financial risk faced by a firm.

Decentralized organization. An approach to managing a large organization by dividing it into units and unit managers' responsibility for the performance of the units. Decentralized organizations require a sophisticated management control system.

Demand pull. A JIT production scheduling concept whereby products are not produced until there is customer demand for the product. Thus, demand "pulls" the production process.

Direct labor. Manufacturing employees who are immediately involved in making a product. Assembly workers are an example. Direct labor occurs only in production departments.

Direct labor budget. A schedule that is part of the operating budget that details the direct labor hours and rate per hour for the budgeted units of production.

Direct labor efficiency variance. The difference between the actual direct labor hours worked and the hours that should have been worked to produce the actual output multiplied by the budgeted (or standard) direct labor pay rate.

Direct labor rate variance. The difference between the actual labor rate paid to employees and the budgeted (or standard) rate that was planned multiplied by the actual hours used.

Direct material. Materials or components that are part of the finished product.

Direct material price variance. The difference between the actual material cost per unit and the budget cost per unit, multiplied by the actual quantity of materials used.

Direct material usage variance. The difference between the quantity of materials used in production and the materials that should have been used to produce the actual output, multiplied by the budgeted material cost per unit.

Discretionary cost center. A department or other area that is not critical to the current operations of the organization. These cost centers perform functions that benefit the firm in the long term. Examples include research and development, advertising, maintenance, and employee development. Performance of discretionary cost centers is difficult to evaluate using financial data.

Economic order quantity (EOQ). The optimum quantity of a part or material to purchase at one time. The EOQ minimizes the total order and carrying costs related to a purchased part or material.

Enterprise resource planning (ERP) software. Software that integrates accounting and other information from most functional areas of the firm. Modules include accounting, marketing, production, and human resources. Examples include SAP, Oracle, and Great Plains.

Ethics. The moral principles that determine the "rightness" or "wrongness" of human behavior.

Exchange gain or loss. Also know as transaction gains or losses. The gain or loss that arises when the time at which a foreign currency transaction is recorded is different from the time cash payment is received or made. The gain or loss occurs because exchange rates change during the time a receivable or payable exists. For example, if you purchase goods from a foreign vendor on account and pay for them 60 days later, a gain or loss will occur to the extent that the dollar has changed value relative to the currency in which the invoice is denominated.

Exchange rate. The rate at which one currency can be converted into another currency.

External failure costs. Costs incurred due to the discovery of defects by customers. These include warranty, legal liability, and time involved in handling customer complaints. The largest external failure costs, the loss of existing and future customers due to loss of goodwill and reputation, are difficult to measure, and often are not formally reported.

Financial budget. Creation of budgeted financial statements based on the operating and capital budget for the coming period. This budget allows managers to acquire the financial resources needed to implement the operating budget.

Financial performance measures. Process output performance measures based on information collected by a firm's financial and cost accounting systems. Examples include product and department cost information, sales revenue, net income, and return on investment. Most firms rely on these as their primary performance measures.

Finished goods inventory. Units that are completed, but not yet sold. The cost of the units in the finished goods inventory is shown in the current assets section of the balance sheet.

Fixed costs. Costs or expenses which *in total* do not change in proportion to changes in the volume of production or sales. Fixed costs *per unit*, however, change as volume changes. Note that most fixed costs change from period to period; they just do not change in proportion to volume.

Future value. The value at some future date of an amount invested or borrowed today, given a specified interest rate.

Future value factor. The value of $1 plus accumulated interest at some specified time in the future at a specified interest rate. The factor is multiplied by the total dollar amount invested to determine the total future value on an investment.

General and administrative expense budget. This schedule, part of the operating budget, contains all planned costs other than manufacturing, selling, and distribution costs.

Hedge. A financial transaction aimed to reduce risk. Many firms will engage in hedging to reduce the risk of losses due to changes in the valuation of currencies.

Historical exchange rate. The exchange rate in effect when a transaction occurred. For example, if a building was purchased in 1975 by a foreign subsidiary of a U.S. firm, the historical exchange rate for that building is the 1975 rate.

Incremental (out-of-pocket) cost (revenue). The amount a cost (or revenue) changes for a given decision. For example, total material cost will increase if a new order for 100 units is accepted. The amount of increase is the incremental material cost for the 100-unit order.

Indirect labor. All manufacturing employees who are not direct labor. Maintenance workers are an example.

Indirect material. Material used in the production process, but it does not become a part of the finished product. Grease used to lubricate production equipment is an example.

Inflation. A reduction in the amount of goods and services a unit of money will purchase. This is generally the result of governments expanding the money supply too fast.

Internal failure costs. Costs incurred to correct problems detected by inspection, testing, etc. These include the cost of rework, scrap, and downtime due to quality problems.

Internal rate of return. The interest rate that will cause the net present value of an investment to equal zero. It is used to compare the relative profitability of proposed capital projects.

Inventory turnover ratio. Cost of goods sold divided by average inventory. This ratio is a measure of how efficiently a firm uses its inventory. As discussed in Module 2, it also has become a critical measure of operating effectiveness for many firms.

Job. A unique, made-to-order product, or identifiable batch of different items being manufactured.

Job-order cost sheet. A document used to record direct material cost (posted from materials requisition forms), direct labor cost (posted from time tickets), and overhead costs for a job.

Job-order costing. The method of costing products that are produced in batches or are custom made. It is distinguished by the collection of manufacturing costs on job-order cost sheets. The alternative is process costing.

Joint venture. A partnership is a partnership of two or more entities that pool a part of their resources to pursue a new business opportunity.

Just-in-time (JIT) system. A process-oriented system that organizes work into cells and seeks to reduce cycle time and inventories through the use of demand pull, preventive maintenance, and continuous improvement.

Kaizen. The Japanese term for continuous process improvement.

Kanban system. The use of cards passed from operation to operation that signals an employee to begin production. Many firms use this system to implement demand pull.

Key success factors. Those few things that a firm must do well if its strategy is going to be successful. Examples include high quality, cost control, and new product development.

Lean production. A name commonly used to describe firms that have implemented JIT concepts throughout the value chain. Toyota is the original lean production firm.

Liquidity. Refers to how quickly a company can convert its assets to cash and the length of time it takes for its liabilities to mature.

Make-or-buy. A decision in which management decides to make a component or an entire product itself or to purchase it from a supplier.

Management by exception. An approach whereby managers focus attention primarily on events that deviate from the plan. Large variances are important exceptions to review.

Management control system. Organizational structure that encourages individual parts of an organization to work toward common goals. The budgeting and performance evaluation subsystems normally form the heart of the management control system.

Managerial (or management) accounting. The collection, analysis and presentation of information to support managerial decision making.

Manufacturing overhead. Production costs other than direct labor and direct material.

Manufacturing overhead budget. This schedule contains all the planned costs in the factory area other than raw materials and direct labor.

Manufacturing process. A set of related activities that convert material and parts into finished products.

Market value. Amount of money an independent buyer is willing to pay for an asset or for an entire company. This amount is different than the accounting or book value of an asset or company which are based on historical cost.

Markup. The amount that a company adds on to its cost base to cover overhead and profit when computing a target selling price.

Markup percentage. Markup divided by cost base

Material requisition form. A document used to record the type and quantity of materials put into production and the job for which the materials are used.

Materials inventory. This inventory consists of parts and raw material waiting to be used in production departments.

Mixed cost. Cost item that is partially a fixed and partially a variable cost. An example is an electric utility bill, which is based on a flat monthly amount plus a rate per kilowatt hour used.

Multinational corporation. A firm with subsidiaries located in more than one country. These firms tend to be more complex because of currency, legal, and cultural differences between countries.

Multiple performance measures. Used to better capture all dimensions of the activity being evaluated; helps reduce the behavioral problems created by measuring employee performance.

Net income. A firm's total sales revenue less its total expenses for the period (year, month, etc.). It is also referred to as net profit, profit, earnings or income.

Net present value. The difference between the present values of cash disbursements and cash receipts for a project.

Nonfinancial measures of performance. Process output performance measures based on information collected outside of traditional accounting systems. These measures are used extensively by firms employing TQM and JIT to provide appropriate incentives for employees. Examples include defect rates, cycle time, and training hours.

Nonmonetary assets. All assets except those defined as monetary. Examples include inventory, equipment and buildings.

Normal cost system. A product costing system in which a firm uses *actual* direct material and *actual* direct labor costs, but employs a *predetermined* overhead rate to cost products. CCC uses a normal cost system.

Operating budget. A detailed plan showing how many units of each product will be produced in which departments, how much material needs to be purchased, how much labor must be hired, etc.

Operations management. The study of how work is organized to meet the goals of an organization.

Ordinary annuity. A series of equal cash flows that are received or paid at the end of each time period in the series.

Overapplied (underapplied) overhead. When overhead applied to the jobs for the period is more (less) than actual overhead cost.

Overhead (or service) department. A manufacturing department that is not a production department. Overhead departments do not work directly on products. Maintenance is an example.

Paradigm. A personal perspective from which events are viewed. An example is a flat versus a global earth perspective.

Participative (budgeting). The involvement of those who will be held accountable for the budget in the development of their budget. It also requires agreement or "buy in" by those held accountable.

Payback period. The time (normally in years) it takes to get your investment back. If cash inflows are the same each year, the formula is initial investment ÷ annual cash inflows.

Performance (also control or flexible) budget. A planning or static budget that has been revised by using actual instead of planned volumes. It is used as the standard against which actual performance is compared.

Performance report. An accounting report showing the performance budget, actual results, and variances.

Period cost. A cost that accountants match to revenue on the income statement by time period. All selling and administrative costs are period costs. No manufacturing costs are period costs.

Planning. The management function of selecting goals, predicting results of specified plans, and deciding how to attain the selected goals.

Planning (static) budget. A budget that is prepared before the year (or other period) begins that is used for planning, motivational, coordinating, and communication purposes, but not for performance evaluation.

Plantwide overhead rate. Overhead allocation procedure whereby all manufacturing overhead costs are collected into one cost pool and allocated to products using one cost driver (usually direct labor hours).

Predetermined overhead rate. A rate computed before the year begins by dividing estimated annual overhead cost by the estimated volume of the cost driver used (direct labor hours in Module 1). This rate is used to apply overhead costs to jobs in work-in-process inventory.

Present value. The value today of an amount to be received or paid at some future date, given a specified interest or discount rate.

Present value factor. The value today of $1 received at some specified time in the future discounted at a specified interest rate. The factor is multiplied by the total dollar amount received in the future to determine the total present value on an investment.

Present value of a lump sum. The value today of a one-time receipt or disbursement of cash at some point in the future discounted at some rate.

Present value of an annuity. The value today of a stream of equal cash receipts or disbursements spread over future periods discounted at some rate.

Prevention costs. Costs incurred to prevent defects. These include product design review, statistical process control, preventive maintenance, employee quality training, and vendor planning and production review costs.

Preventive maintenance. A JIT concept stipulating that factory operators be trained and held responsible for maintaining their equipment.

Process. A series of related activities or steps focused on achieving a specified output. Examples of processes at CCC are manufacturing, new product development, and billing and collection.

Process costing. Method of costing used when only one product or a family of similar products are produced on one set of equipment. It averages all costs across all units produced in the period.

Process output measures. Measures developed by accountants from key success factors. They are used to monitor how well each process contributes to a firm's success. These measures are part of the management control system.

Process quality improvement. A generic term used to describe any methodology used to improve process quality. Examples include total quality management and Six Sigma.

Product cost. A cost that accountants match to revenue on the income statement by products sold. These costs can be inventoried (work-in-process and finished goods). All manufacturing costs are product costs.

Production budget. A schedule that contains the projected units to be produced for the coming period. It uses information from the sales budget and takes into consideration beginning and ending finished goods inventories for the budget period.

Production department. A department that works directly on a product. The alternative is an overhead department.

Production process. The sequence of events involved in physically manufacturing products. The process involves all the manufacturing activities necessary to complete a product including the delivery of materials and the cutting, assembly, finishing, and inspection of units.

Purchases budget. A schedule that details the quantity of materials a firm must buy to meet its budget, considering the effects of both the planned beginning and ending material inventories.

Random fluctuations. Normal variations from the mean that occur in a process that is under statistical control. There are no explanations for these fluctuations other than that they are a natural result of the process.

Relevant cost. A cost that is incremental to a decision under study; that is, it will change if the alternative under review is implemented. Direct material cost in a special order decision is an example.

Relevant range. The range of operating activity (units produced) over which total fixed costs remain constant. This is usually the normal operating range of volume for a firm.

Responsibility accounting (reporting). A performance evaluation system, based on the budget, that holds responsibility center managers accountable for those areas over which they have control.

Responsibility center. A unit of an organization that holds its managers accountable for specific activities and outcomes that may included costs, revenues, or profits.

Return on equity ratio. Net income divided by average stockholders' equity. This ratio is a measure of how much the company is earning for stockholders relative to the amount of investment made by stockholders. The higher a firm's ROE, the better it is performing for stockholders.

Return on sales ratio. Net income divided by net sales (total sales less sales returns and allowances). This ratio, also known as the net profit margin, is an overall measure of a firm's relative profitability. For example, If firm A has a return on sales of .05 and Firm B in the same industry has an operating performance ratio of .10, it means Firm B earns twice the profit on each dollar of sales revenue as firm A. All other things being equal, Firm B will earn a higher return on equity.

Sales budget. A schedule that contains planned unit sales and prices by product, by territory, and by other desired segments.

Sales revenue. The total amount a firm charges for goods and services sold during the period (month, year, etc.). Also referred to simply as sales or revenue.

Salvage (or residual) value. The amount received (or estimated to be received at a future date) when a long-lived asset is sold or scrapped.

Selling and distribution expense budget. A schedule that contains all the planned costs of marketing, selling, and distributing the product or service to customers.

Settlement date. The date at which a liability is paid.

Six Sigma. A process management system with the objective to build quality into processes to the extent that each activity will have a defect rate of less than 3.4 defects per million.

Special cause events. An event that impacts the operation of an activity, but is external to the normal operation of that activity. An earthquake that causes large fluctuations in machine tolerance is an example.

Special order. The one-time sale of goods or services to a non-regular customer below the normal selling price.

Standard cost. Estimates made before the year begins of how much an item should cost.

Standards. Estimate made before the period begins on quantity, rate, or cost of an activity. If a standard is a cost, it is termed a *standard cost*. Other examples of standards include the number of pounds of material per unit of product and the expected defect rate.

Statistical quality control. The use of statistics, including control charts, to improve the quality of products or services.

Strategic planning. A description of how a firm plans to attain its goals. It includes the markets in which a firm will operate, the type of products or services it will sell, the pricing it will use, and the technologies it will employ.

Suboptimization. A systems concept stating that optimizing the individual parts of a system will not optimize the entire system. Traditional management control systems focus on the optimization of individual department performance, thereby causing suboptimization.

Sunk cost. A cost stemming from a past decision, which cannot be changed by decisions made today. A sunk cost is not relevant to decision about the future. An example is a past investment in a building.

Supply chain management. The integration of suppliers, producers and distributors of goods or services to minimize cost and optimize service. The essence of supply chain management is to have independent companies integrate their information systems to improve decision making.

Support process. A process that is not part of the value chain, but supports it. Examples include billing and collection, planning, and information systems processes.

Tampering. Attempts by management to improve a process by using common cause variations as a basis for action. Tampering only increases process variation.

Target cost. A pricing technique that begins by determining what customers will pay for a product and works back to an allowable cost for manufacturing the product. It is basically the reverse of cost-plus pricing.

Target price. The price at which a firm would like to sell its products or services so that all costs and an acceptable profit margin are covered. The firm may actually price the goods or services higher or lower based on market considerations.

Target rate of return. The rate of return a firm desires to obtain when investing in new projects.

Time ticket. A document used to record the number of hours a direct labor person worked on each job during a day.

Time value of money. The concept that money changes in value with time because it earns interest. For example, receiving money today is preferable to receiving the same amount of money at some later date because the money received today and invested will earn interest.

Total quality management. A management philosophy that focuses on the customer, processes, process variation, and measurement.

Trade balance of payments surplus (deficit). When the value of goods and services exported is greater (less) than the value of goods and services imported.

Traditional overhead allocation. Allocation of overhead based on one or more drivers that are highly correlated with production volume (for example, direct labor hours). Overhead allocation in Module 1 is an example of traditional, volume-based overhead allocation.

Transfer pricing. Determining the price charged for the purchase of goods or services by one business unit by another business unit within the same company. Transfer prices are an important issue for decentralized organizations.

Translation. The process of converting the financial statements of a foreign subsidiary into the currency used by the parent company.

Translation gains (losses). The increase (decrease) in the book value of a foreign subsidiary due to changes in exchange rates during the period.

Underapplied overhead. See overapplied overhead.

Under(over)-costed products. Assignment of less (more) overhead to a product than production of that product caused. Activity-Based costing reduces the under- and over-costing of products by more accurately assigning overhead to products.

Value-added activity. An activity that, from the customers' perspective, is worth more than the cost of that activity. Work-in-process inventory normally is a non-value-added activity because customers won't pay more for products just because a firm maintains high work-in-process inventories.

Value chain. Set of interdependent processes that add value, from the customer's perspective, to a product or service. In the value chain, the process normally includes research and development, product design, manufacturing, distribution and customer service.

Variable costs. Costs that change *in total* in proportion to changes in the volume of production or sales. Variable costs *per unit* remain constant as volume changes.

Variance. The difference between the performance (flexible) budget and actual results.

Variation. Differences in products or services that are produced in the same process. In the view of TQM advocates, the lower the variation, the higher the quality.

Work cell. An area of a factory dedicated to producing one product or a family of similar products. It contains different types of equipment that perform different steps in the production process.

Work-in-process inventory. This inventory consists of all of a firm's partially completed units. The cost of these units is shown as a current asset on the balance sheet.